Understanding Early Years Theory in Practice

Maureen Daly

Elisabeth Byers

Wendy Taylor

www.heinemann.co.uk
✓ Free online support
✓ Useful weblinks
✓ 24 hour online ordering

01865 888058

Heinemann

Inspiring generations

Heinemann Educational Publishers
Halley Court, Jordan Hill, Oxford OX2 8EJ
Part of Harcourt Education

Heinemann is the registered trademark of
Harcourt Education Limited

Text © Maureen Daly, Elisabeth Byers, Wendy Taylor 2006

First published 2006

10 09 08 07 06
10 9 8 7 6 5 4 3 2 1

British Library Cataloguing in Publication Data is available
from the British Library on request.

10-digit ISBN: 0 435402137
13-digit ISBN: 978 0 435402 13 6

Typeset and illustrated by Saxon Graphics Ltd, Derby
Original illustrations © Harcourt Education Limited, 2006
Cover design by Wooden Ark Studio, Leeds
Printed in the UK by Bath Press
Cover photo: © Zefa

Acknowledgements
Every effort has been made to contact copyright holders of material reproduced in this book.
Any omissions will be rectified in subsequent printings if notice is given to the publishers.

The author and publisher would like to thank Sheila Riddall-Leech for permission to use the
appendix.

Photo acknowledgements
Page 3: Harcourt Ltd / Jules Selmes; page 15: Corbis / Bettmann; page 21: AKG Images; page 34:
Forestry Commission / Isobel Cameron; page 42: Corbis / Bettmann; page 43: Corbis / Laura
Dwight; page 58: Topham Picturepoint; page 63: Topham Picturepoint; page 65: Elisabeth Byers;
page 75: Getty Images Editorial; page 76: Getty Images / AFP; page 80: Photos.com; page 86:
Alamy Images / Pegaz; page 93: Harcourt Ltd / Jules Selmes; page 110: Corbis / Stefano Bianchetti;
page 117 top: Tudor Photography, bottom: Photos.com; page 118 top: Corbis / Laura Dwight,
middle: Harcourt Ltd / Jules Selmes, bottom: Photofusion; page 119: Lucinda Douglas-Menzies /
National Portrait Gallery, London; page 120: Corbis / Steve Prezant; page 132: Brand X Pictures;
page 155: Elisabeth Byers; page 160: Science Photo Library; page 161: Corbis / Bettmann; page
162: Corbis / Roger Ressmeyer; page 169: AKG Images; page 174: National Portrait Gallery,
London; page 176: Topham Picturepoint

Contents

Acknowledgements   v

About the authors   vi

Introduction   vii

Chapter 1   Children's learning frameworks   1
             Curriculum frameworks   2
             Other learning frameworks   15

Chapter 2   How children learn   41
             The work of theorists and researchers on how children learn 42
             The role of the early years practitioner in promoting learning 67

Chapter 3   Children's communication   73
             How children learn to speak   74
             The importance of early social interaction   81
             Supporting children in early literacy   88

Chapter 4   Children's relationships   107
             The child as a social being   108
             Constructing first relationships   116
             The beginnings of friendship and the growth of intimacy   128
             The key person approach   134
             Transference   136

Chapter 5   How children feel   141
             Emotional intelligence   143
             Sense of self   152
             Self-esteem   153
             Coping with feelings   155
             How adults interact with children   158
             Key theories about how children feel   159

Chapter 6	**Children's play**	**167**
	The pioneers of the early years curriculum	168
	Tina Bruce and free-flow play	177
	Pulling the theories together	179
	Adult-initiated play and child-initiated play	183
	Structured play	188
	The play environment	190
	Heuristic play	194
	Outdoor play	196
Glossary		201
Appendix		205
Index		211

Acknowledgements

I would like to thank my niece Laura for just 'being herself' and my family for all their patience. I would also like to say a special thanks to my fellow authors and publisher Beth Howard for their continued support.

Maureen Daly

I would like to thank Joseph and Peter for their endless patience during the writing of this book and my fellow authors for their endless childcare wisdom and constant inspiration. I also thank Beth for her encouragement and guidance.

Elisabeth Byers

I would like to thank my family, who have put up with me spending my time being 'bookish' again for several months, particularly Kevin, Leza and Adam who suffer the most. I am also indebted to work colleagues and students for reading parts of the book in various stages and for contributing ideas and knowledge: Brigid Osgood, Caroline Chalke, Mary Plows, Vicky Brooker, Karen Conroy and the DCE year 2 students from Oaklands College. Galina Dolya and David Higgins from Shining Eyes and Busy Minds have also been very supportive and helpful with their knowledge of the work of Lev Vygotsky.

The whole project took a lot of effort and my contribution would not have been finished without Maureen, Lizzie and Beth Howard from Heinemann who always has such faith in us.

Finally I would like to mention Katie Wilkinson – a beautiful person whose death had a big impact on our family while this book was being written.

Wendy Taylor

About the authors

Maureen Daly

Maureen Daly spent over 20 years working in a variety of early years settings and also managed an early years establishment. She has been a lecturer in early years in colleges of further education, teaching on a variety of courses in childcare and education at all levels. Since 2001 she has worked at Oaklands College, where she has been Curriculum Leader in Care and Early Years, Programme Leader for the Sector Endorsed Foundation Degree in Childhood Studies and Coordinator of the Centre of Vocational Excellence. For the last three years she has also been an External Moderator for awarding body CACHE.

Elisabeth Byers

Elisabeth Byers qualified as a nursery nurse and then started her career in the United States, where she worked in a kindergarten and in a hospital for sick children as a volunteer. She returned to the UK to work in a school, when she worked with nursery, reception and year 1 children, and became involved in managing an out-of-school club. In addition to this she worked as supply cover for day care centres, when she worked with 0–5-year-olds. She has been teaching at Oaklands College in Hertfordshire since 1998 on a range of early years courses, including those leading to the CCE, DCE, NVQ and Foundation Degree qualifications. As Coordinator for Early Years Placements she is responsible for managing the placement process for each student.

Wendy Taylor

Wendy Taylor has been involved in childcare and education since 1977. She originally trained as an early years teacher at the University of East Anglia. She moved into pre-school work after the birth of her children, and eventually managed her own setting. She has worked at Oaklands College for 10 years, training classroom assistants, nursery nurses, nannies, childminders, babysitters and pre-school workers. She is Coordinator of the CACHE Diploma in Childcare and Education and a Teaching and Learning Leader. She has also assessed settings for the Herts Quality Standards Accreditation Scheme.

Introduction

It takes a lot of experience and patience to understand children with any real depth and good practitioners know that they will continue to learn about children's development and learning throughout their careers. The UK government's strategy to build a highly skilled early years workforce means that you need to be well-trained and constantly developing your skills. You will need to have an excellent understanding of child development, care and education, and of the theories which underpin good practice in order to be a reflective practitioner.

Reflective practice is key to you being able to evaluate your own effectiveness in relation to what you understand about the theories of children's development and learning. It is part of an ongoing process of self-assessment that occurs throughout your career and requires practice and an open-minded approach. Reflective practitioners are able to:

- take responsibility for the way they work
- critically evaluate their own work
- build upon their own experiences to the benefit of the child
- think about the effect of their planning and actions on the child's learning
- improve practice
- actively challenge accepted practice if they don't think it benefits the child
- question whether children's real needs are being met
- question whether the children are being challenged and stimulated
- alter their approach in order to improve things for the child
- interpret events in relation to their understanding of child development theory.

The purpose of this book is to provide an accessible account for early years students who are working at level 3 and also for existing practitioners and students on a level 4 course who wish to revisit their knowledge and understanding. Early years tutors and practitioners will find the book a useful resource and a prompt for discussion about how children learn and the implications of theoretical perspectives for modern practice. The authors, as experienced childcare tutors, recognise the challenges that many students and practitioners face in linking theoretical perspectives to their own work with children. These challenges can be:

◆ experiencing difficulty in understanding the theory and terminology used – What does that mean?

◆ difficulty in applying the theory to practice – What difference does that make to my work?

◆ recognising the importance of theory – Why do I need to know that?

The book therefore makes frequent reference to real-life examples to help you relate theories of children's development and learning to your practice. Underpinning each chapter is an explanation of:

◆ why it is important to understand the theoretical aspects of early years practice

◆ the benefit to children of the experiences offered in early years settings

◆ your role in supporting children's development and learning.

The work of researchers and theorists helps you to continually develop and evaluate children's development. Throughout this book we have endeavoured to present established and emerging theory in an accessible way. Each chapter looks at different aspects of the child's development and relates theory to current practice with an emphasis on your role in providing relevant learning and development opportunities.

◆ **Chapter 1** sets the scene by outlining the current National Curriculum and learning frameworks and considers the other styles of provision which influence practice. The chapter looks closely at the Curriculum Guidance for the Foundation Stage and the Birth to Three Matters Framework, and outlines the practical applications of these and the principles underpinning them. Consideration is also given to the work of Maria Montessori and Rudolf Steiner, with clear explanations of the key focus of their work and the way this is interpreted in Montessori and Steiner schools today. Some elements of these approaches are also used in mainstream education and this is also true of the other two approaches discussed in the remainder of the chapter. The Reggio Emilia approach from Italy has been adapted for use in pre-school settings and has provoked much discussion of the exciting elements fundamental to the approach, such as the use of the expressive arts and the environment to foster learning and development in young children. The ideas of the Forest Schools, to use the outdoor environment and to encourage the children in independence, are also looked at closely and practical applications considered.

◆ **Chapter 2** focuses on children's ability to learn and looks closely at the work of Jean Piaget and Lev Vygotsky. The main features of their theories are described and discussed in the context of modern practice. Both theorists have had a significant influence on the way practitioners approach the education of young children and you are encouraged to think about this in detail in relation to your own practice. The work of Jerome Bruner relates to the theories he has identified of scaffolding learning for children and the importance of the adult role in providing appropriate learning experiences.

The chapter also discusses the identification of schemas in relation to Piaget. Modern-day research on this fascinating aspect of the way children learn is discussed through the work of Tina Bruce and the Pen Green Centre.

The remainder of this chapter reflects on your role in interpreting and applying these theoretical perspectives.

◆ **Chapter 3** explores the way in which children communicate, including theories relating to the acquisition of speech, the importance of early social interaction and how to support children's early literacy. You will need to record the language development of young children, so it is vital that you understand how children learn to speak and acquire language skills. One of your challenges is to encourage early writing skills by using the environment and examples of print all around us. We consider good practice in this area to give ideas for support. There is a vast amount written about the acquisition of language and supporting children through this vital area of development and skill. It can be concluded that a child who is stimulated from an early age with rich interactions and warm relationships will be able to take on the immense task of learning to speak, read and write. You play an essential part in this development and need to have the correct resources and skills to motivate and encourage young children. Much of the research we will look at has shown that listening to children is pivotal. After all – we expect them to listen to us!

◆ **Chapter 4** discusses some of the key theorists in social development. You need to understand the importance of the social development of children, firstly looking at their place in society and considering some of the expectations of family and culture. We discuss some of the key theorists in social development, looking at how children construct their first relationships and form attachments with their mothers. It is vital that you have an in-depth knowledge of how children find their place in society and how they construct their earliest relationships. With this knowledge and understanding, you can support both the child and the adults around them to gain the very best from their relationships and interactions with people close to them and in the wider world.

◆ **Chapter 5** considers children's healthy emotional development and covers the work of Carl Rogers, Sigmund Freud and John Bowlby. From birth, children rapidly develop their ability to experience and express different emotions as well as their capacity to cope with and manage a variety of feelings. Most of these capabilities are in place by the time children are 2 years old. Therefore it is vital for practitioners working with very young children to have a sound understanding of the process of emotional development and the influences that may impact on children's emotional health. Emotions affect our social behaviour and many of the choices we make are also influenced by emotions. Learning to manage feelings and emotions can be very difficult for some children and can result in future psychological difficulties if not appropriately supported early on by the adults around them.

♦ **Chapter 6** looks at children's play and the variety of ways in which play supports children's learning. Free-flow play, structured play and play environments are considered. Theory and research indicates that one of the greatest attributes of play is that it supports children's learning in a variety of ways. Many early years practitioners recognise the value of play. However, it seems that play is not necessarily utilised as an effective method of learning in all settings.

Throughout, the focus of the book is on the ideas of key theorists and theoretical perspectives, with a variety of features included to help you relate this to your practice:

♦ **Case study** – real-life scenarios demonstrating theory in practice

♦ **Think about it** – ideas and thought-provoking questions to help you recognise the theory in your practice

♦ **Try it out** – suggested tasks and activities to help you put what they have learned into practice

♦ **Good practice checklist** – useful checklists of important points for best practice

♦ **Check your understanding** – short-answer questions at the end of each chapter to check understanding and review what has just been covered

♦ **References** – a list of suggested sources of further information at the end of each chapter for those who want to explore a theory in more depth

♦ **Glossary** – a list of key terms at the end of the book.

To help readers who are searching for information on a particular theorist, each chapter begins with a list of all theorists discussed in that chapter with page numbers provided for quick reference.

Chapter 1

Children's learning frameworks

Introduction

In early years, there are a number of different types of setting and provision for the education and care of young children. These range from the traditional school setting and state-funded nurseries to the privately-owned day care establishments. Within this spectrum of provision, there are curriculum and learning frameworks, which structure the environment and experiences for children to give them the best possible start in life. These frameworks also provide a standard for the education of children, with the focus on ensuring that every child has an equal opportunity to learn.

In recent years these frameworks have included the nationally agreed curriculum: the National Curriculum for 5–16-year-olds, the Curriculum Guidance for the Foundation Stage for 3–5-year-olds and the Birth to Three Matters Framework for the very youngest children. In addition to the legislative curriculum, other learning frameworks are also used and for the purposes of this book we have chosen to discuss frameworks based on the work of the pioneers **Maria Montessori** and **Rudolf Steiner**. Although both lived and worked many years ago, their ideas and philosophies are still very relevant today. Many private schools exist throughout the world that reflect their respective ideologies, and modern-day practitioners are interested in the impact they have on children's learning, particularly as many parents choose to send their children to Montessori or Steiner schools in their pre-school years before starting state education.

In addition, this chapter considers the Reggio Emilia approach to early years education and the Forest Schools from Sweden and Denmark. The work of educators in the Italian town of Reggio Emilia has caused a stir throughout the world and has proved to be a focus for educators in the UK to reflect on the quality of their own provision. Many of the ideas and practices have been adopted within settings and it is therefore relevant to discuss this approach within this chapter. The Forest Schools are relatively new to the UK with most of the pioneering work being carried out by Bridgwater College in Somerset. However, the ideas are spreading and reflect current views on the importance of the outdoor curriculum in children's learning.

This chapter covers:

◆ Curriculum frameworks

◆ Other learning frameworks.

The theorists covered in this chapter are:

◆ **Maria Montessori**, page 15

◆ **Rudolf Steiner**, page 21.

Curriculum frameworks

Curriculum Guidance for the Foundation Stage

The Curriculum Guidance for the Foundation Stage, for children aged 3–5, was introduced in September 2000 and was an important landmark in funded education in England. For the first time, this stage of education had its own identity and curriculum guidance.

Principles

The Curriculum Guidance is based upon the principles of good and effective practice for early years education listed below.

GOOD PRACTICE CHECKLIST

Principles of good practice in the Curriculum Guidance for the Foundation Stage

◆ Effective education requires a relevant curriculum and practitioners who understand and are able to implement the curriculum requirements.

◆ Effective education requires practitioners who understand that children develop rapidly during the early years – physically, intellectually, emotionally and socially.

◆ Practitioners should ensure that all children feel included, secure and valued.

◆ Early years experience should build on what children already know and can do.

◆ No child should be excluded or disadvantaged.

◆ Parents and practitioners should work together.

◆ An early years curriculum should be carefully structured.

◆ There should be opportunities for children to engage in activities planned by adults and also those that they plan or initiate themselves.

◆ Practitioners must be able to observe and respond appropriately to children.

◆ Well-planned, purposeful activity and appropriate intervention by practitioners will engage children in the learning process.

◆ The learning environment should be well planned and well organised.

◆ The care and education by practitioners should be high-quality.

Source: Adapted from DfES (2000), pages 11 and 12

The Curriculum Guidance is based upon the principles of good and effective practice for early years education

THINK ABOUT IT

Consider these principles in relation to your own practice and the setting in which you work. Reflect on the impact these principles have.

Some of the issues you may have considered are set out in the table below.

Curriculum Guidance for the Foundation Stage: impact on practice

Principles for early years education	Impact on practice
Effective education requires a relevant curriculum and practitioners who understand and are able to implement the curriculum requirements.	You need to have a good knowledge of the Curriculum Guidance for the Foundation Stage and the activities you plan for the children should be based on this. You will need to discuss with colleagues how to implement this effectively. This can be achieved through regular planning sessions to devise long-, medium- and short-term plans that reflect appropriate activities for children and that encourage progression through the stepping stones. You will also need to attend regular courses related to the areas of learning so that you continue to provide stimulating experiences for the children and can disseminate new ideas to your colleagues.

Effective education requires practitioners who understand that children develop rapidly during the early years – physically, intellectually, emotionally and socially.	You need to have an excellent understanding of child development in all areas – physical, intellectual, emotional and social – and know how to challenge children and promote their development. This may entail regular updating of knowledge, discussion with colleagues and recognition of staff training needs. Settings will also need to have quality assurance schemes in place to ensure that standards are maintained and children are given equal opportunity to progress.
Practitioners should ensure that all children feel included, secure and valued.	You should ensure all children in the setting feel a part of it and are comfortable there. You may do this by putting up displays with the children and using equipment that reflects the community and wider world. Children and their families must be welcomed to the setting and their home life and culture respected and valued. Settings should use a key worker system, where one adult is responsible for a small group of children, to help children feel more secure, and the children's views and needs should be valued and listened to.
Early years experience should build on what children already know and can do.	You will need to build a picture of the child's capabilities and needs. Many settings arrange home visits that give staff an opportunity to talk to the child and parent in their own home before they start at the setting. It is also a good idea to spend time talking to parents about the child so that activities can be provided that reflect the children's interests and experience and build upon their existing knowledge. You will need to observe children in order to determine their level of understanding and to plan progression activities. These observations should be shared with the rest of the team and the parents in order to work together to extend learning for the child.

No child should be excluded or disadvantaged.	You must look carefully at the materials and equipment available for the children to use and ensure they do not exclude or disadvantage children, for example appropriate scissors provided for children who are left-handed, enough craft equipment for the number of children involved in the activity, equal chances to do special activities, such as cooking, and adaptations to equipment for children who have difficulties. You need to know the individual needs of the children in your care in order to make sure they have equal opportunity. Every child's needs must be taken into account when planning activities and experiences in order to ensure equality of opportunity.
Parents and practitioners should work together.	This could involve parents' evenings, home–school books, parents helping in the classroom, fathers' mornings, social events and information evenings.
An early years curriculum should be carefully structured.	You should plan activities for the children linking them to the expectations of achievement for children of that age and stage of development. Plans should be made for the whole year and then broken down into topics, weekly and daily plans. Experiences provided should be rich and varied and stimulate learning, and should include the use of the outdoor environment. Regular observations of the children must be carried out to ensure that all children are accessing quality activities and experiences that reflect the aims of the Curriculum Guidance for the Foundation Stage.

There should be opportunities for children to engage in activities planned by adults and also those that they plan or initiate themselves.	Some activities will be specifically planned by staff to reflect the early learning goals, such as opportunities for mark-making, drawing and painting, learning nursery rhymes, listening to stories in a group. You should also allow children to develop their own ideas and follow their interests as this stimulates learning and independence. Children learn from organising their own games, taking part in imaginative play and coming up with their own ideas.
Practitioners must be able to observe and respond appropriately to children.	You will be involved in writing detailed observations on the children that are then shared with colleagues and used to plan appropriate activities for the children to follow. The observations can be kept in a portfolio and shared with parents and children, forming links between school and home. Observations give you the chance to learn about the children in your care and to respond appropriately to their needs, to note their progress in relation to expectations and to relate this to theories of development. Observations should use different methods, for example narrative, charts and checklists, to obtain as much information as possible. The use of observations provides a basis for assessment and portfolios of these built up over the course of the Foundation Stage enable you to establish the Foundation Stage Profile at the end of the child's time in the Foundation Stage.

Well-planned, purposeful activity and appropriate intervention by practitioners will engage children in the learning process.	You need to make sure the children are involved in interesting and challenging activities that promote learning. You will need to know when to intervene in children's play and when to let it flow naturally by carefully observing the pattern of the play and the learning that is taking place. Intervention will be necessary for health and safety reasons or if a child is being disadvantaged by the play or behaviour of others. It may also be necessary to intervene in order to extend the play. You should do this by sensitively involving yourself in the play situation. It is important not to dominate the play but to take cues from the children.
The learning environment should be well planned and well organised.	The equipment should be accessible to the children so that they can choose materials to play with by providing cupboards and drawers the children can reach. Equipment should be kept in the same place so children know where everything is and where to return it to. The environment should reflect a variety of stimulating and exciting experiences and give children the space to play together. Some areas should remain the same, for example the water and sand play, to provide security and reassurance and any changes to the environment should be done slowly and sensitively. Children can be involved in planning, such as the imaginative play area with regular changes of focus from hairdressers to a pirate ship, a house to a hot air balloon basket. It is important to maintain a tidy and clean environment with old displays taken down when they become tatty and all children having some of their work displayed over the course of the year. The children can be encouraged to take part in this with a specific 'tidy-up time' – sometimes when the music goes on.

The care and education by practitioners should be high-quality.	Your work should reflect the high importance of the task of looking after young children. You need to be aware of what constitutes good practice and have the best interests of the child in mind at all times. Quality assurance schemes should be introduced.

Meeting children's needs

Throughout the Curriculum Guidance for the Foundation Stage, there is a strong emphasis on the need to provide activities and experiences that challenge children and promote development through meeting individual and diverse needs. Every child that starts at an early years setting comes with different experiences, skills and knowledge and ability to learn. You have to plan their provision in a way that meets the needs of every individual whatever their background, race, gender or need. This is not always easy, but the Curriculum Guidance highlights key expectations for doing this:

◆ 'Plan opportunities that build on and extend children's knowledge, experiences, interests and skills and develop their self-esteem and confidence in their ability to learn.

◆ Use a wide range of teaching strategies, based on children's learning needs.

◆ Provide a range of opportunities to motivate, support and develop children and help them to be involved, concentrate and learn effectively.

◆ Provide a safe and supportive learning environment, free from harassment, in which the contribution of all children is valued and where racial, religious, disability and gender stereotypes are challenged.

◆ Use materials that positively reflect diversity and are free from discrimination and stereotyping.

◆ Plan challenging opportunities for children whose ability and understanding are in advance of their language and communication skills.

◆ Monitor children's progress, identifying any areas for concern, and taking action to provide support, for example by using different approaches, additional adult help or other agencies.'

Source: DfES (2000), pages 17–18

The principles for early education and the expectations for meeting children's diverse needs underpin good practice in any setting and are assessed by the Ofsted inspection process.

Areas of learning

There are six key areas of learning identified by the Curriculum Guidance that assist practitioners in their planning of the learning environment and provide a framework for the early years curriculum. These are outlined in the table below.

Curriculum Guidance for the Foundation Stage: areas of learning

Area of learning	Key features
Personal, social and emotional development	◆ Relationships ◆ Independence ◆ Respect for self and others ◆ Self-image ◆ Friendships ◆ Positive approach to learning ◆ Role-models ◆ Feelings
Communication, language and literacy	◆ Communication of thoughts, ideas and feelings ◆ Building relationships ◆ Interaction ◆ Rhymes, music, songs, poetry, stories and non-fiction books ◆ Writing ◆ Reading ◆ Spoken language ◆ Conversations ◆ Alternative communication systems, e.g. sign language ◆ Listening
Mathematical development	◆ Numbers ◆ Patterns ◆ Counting ◆ Calculating ◆ Shape, space, measure
Knowledge and understanding of the world	◆ Basis for science, design and technology, history, geography and information and communication technology (ICT) ◆ Exploration ◆ Observation ◆ Problem-solving ◆ Prediction ◆ Critical thinking ◆ Decision-making ◆ Discussion ◆ Curiosity ◆ Questioning

Physical development	◆ Improving skills ◆ Co-ordination ◆ Control ◆ Manipulation ◆ Movement ◆ Confidence ◆ Health ◆ Active ◆ Challenging ◆ Indoors and outdoors space
Creative development	◆ Art ◆ Music ◆ Dance ◆ Role play ◆ Imaginative play ◆ Originality ◆ Exploration and experimentation with materials ◆ Learning through the senses ◆ Ideas

The impact of the areas of learning has been significant for settings. All early years settings now conduct their planning based on these six areas. For example, many settings use topics to organise the children's learning for the year and each topic will be divided into activities that promote the six areas. Outcomes for the children's learning will be identified based on the stepping stones (see below) as set out in the Curriculum Guidance for the Foundation Stage. Practitioners ensure that equal emphasis is given to each area of learning to make sure children have a balanced curriculum.

> ### TRY IT OUT
>
> *Look at each area of learning for the Foundation Stage.*
> *Consider the equipment and activities available in your setting for the children to use.*
> *Which area/areas of learning do they promote?*

The areas of learning for the Foundation Stage are divided into early learning goals, which are the established expectations for children to achieve. Stepping stones are identified in the Curriculum Guidance to help you devise activities that will enable children to reach the early learning goals. These stepping stones are colour-coded, with those most easily achieved being yellow, through blue and green to the grey band of the early learning goal. The Guidance also includes examples of what children can do and what you need to help the assessment of the child's skills and to teach progression.

Look at a copy of the Curriculum Guidance for the Foundation Stage. All early years settings should have copies, or you can obtain your own (see References, page 39).

1 Read through the file carefully and familiarise yourself with the areas of learning and the early learning goals.

2 In discussion with your supervisor or a colleague, decide on an area of learning that the children in your setting are working towards. Discuss the stepping stones that the children will need to progress through in order to reach their goal. What do you need to do? There is guidance for action in the Curriculum.

Birth to Three Matters Framework

This framework for the education and care of children from birth to 3 years works within the context of the Curriculum Guidance for the Foundation Stage and the National Standards for Under Eights Day Care and Childminding. It is a framework for any practitioner to use and provides support, information and guidance for individuals and settings. The child is seen as the focus of the framework, rather than subjects or areas of learning, and it emphasises the importance of this age range in its own right. It values and celebrates babies and young children and recognises their individuality and efforts.

Principles

As with the Curriculum Guidance, Birth to Three Matters includes underpinning key principles of good practice, such as those listed below.

GOOD PRACTICE CHECKLIST

Principles of good practice in the Birth to Three Matters Framework

◆ 'Parents and families are central to the well-being of the child.

◆ Relationships with other people are of crucial importance in a child's life.

◆ A relationship with a key person at home and in the setting is essential to young people's well-being.

◆ Babies and young children are social beings; they are competent learners from birth.

◆ Learning is a shared process and children learn most effectively when, with the support of a knowledgeable adult, they are actively involved and interested.

◆ Caring adults count more than resources and equipment.

◆ Schedules and routines must flow with the child's needs.

◆ Children learn when they are given appropriate responsibility, allowed to make errors, decisions and choices, and respected as autonomous and competent learners.

◆ Children learn by doing rather than being told.

◆ Young children are vulnerable. They learn to be independent by having someone they can depend on.'

Source: DfES/Sure Start (2002), pages 4–5

How do these principles impact on practice?

For the first time, a framework has been developed for the youngest children. This recognises the importance of the earliest years of life in determining the long-term well-being and success of the child. It also recognises and values the work being done by practitioners and helps to standardise the care and education that the children are exposed to, ensuring quality in provision whether they live in Cornwall or Yorkshire, Carlisle or Peterborough.

Practitioners have received training through government-sponsored funding and are expected to reflect the framework within their setting through planning and practice. There is clear guidance for practitioners through the booklet, video, and CD-ROM available in the *Birth to Three Matters* pack and component cards which can be displayed within the setting and identify effective practice, play and practical support and meeting diverse needs.

THINK ABOUT IT

Helen's interview

Helen has recently left college having gained a level 3 childcare qualification. She particularly enjoys working with babies and young children and is delighted when she is invited to be interviewed for a post working with children aged 6–12 months.

As part of her interview she has been asked to do a short presentation about the qualities and skills she will need, based on the principles underpinning the Birth to Three Framework.

Look at the principles outlined above. What skills and abilities do you consider are necessary when working with babies and young children?

When you considered the qualities that Helen will need, linked to the principles, you may have thought of the following abilities:

◆ building relationships with children that support and value them and encourage their well-being and trust

◆ forming relationships with parents that are professional and which respect the relationship they have with their child

◆ understanding the developmental needs of babies and young children and how to promote their learning

◆ sharing experiences with children and enjoying them together

◆ being enthusiastic and caring

◆ recognising the vulnerability of young children and being able to encourage them to independence appropriately.

Aspects of the framework

The framework is organised into four aspects of the child:

◆ a Strong Child
◆ a Skilful Communicator
◆ a Competent Learner
◆ a Healthy Child.

The key ideas running through the four aspects are summarised in the table below. Note that adults play an essential role throughout.

Birth to Three Matters Framework: key ideas in the four aspects of the framework

Aspect of the framework	Key ideas
A Strong Child	Children who are strong, capable, confident and self-assured. The baby needs a nurturing, loving environment from which he can make the journey of self-discovery with success. Adults play an essential role.
A Skilful Communicator	Children learning to make sense of the sounds around them and turning these into 'conversations'. Learning the 'rules' of communication, listening and responding and finding a voice. Building social relationships.
A Competent Learner	Making sense of their world through connections of experiences. Exploring the world through their senses, discovering and experimenting.
A Healthy Child	Being cared for so they develop physically, socially and emotionally. Experiencing warm relationships, growing and developing with enthusiasm and energy. Being protected and kept safe.

Each aspect has four components, as shown below. The framework identifies what is included in each aspect and component.

The example below shows how an activity such as using musical instruments with a small group of 1-year-old children can promote and encourage the four aspects of the Birth to Three Matters Framework.

> **TRY IT OUT**
>
> *Consider activities that you provide for young children and how they meet the Birth to Three Framework.*

There are plans to combine the Curriculum Guidance for the Foundation Stage and the Birth to Three Matters Framework in the future to create the Early Years

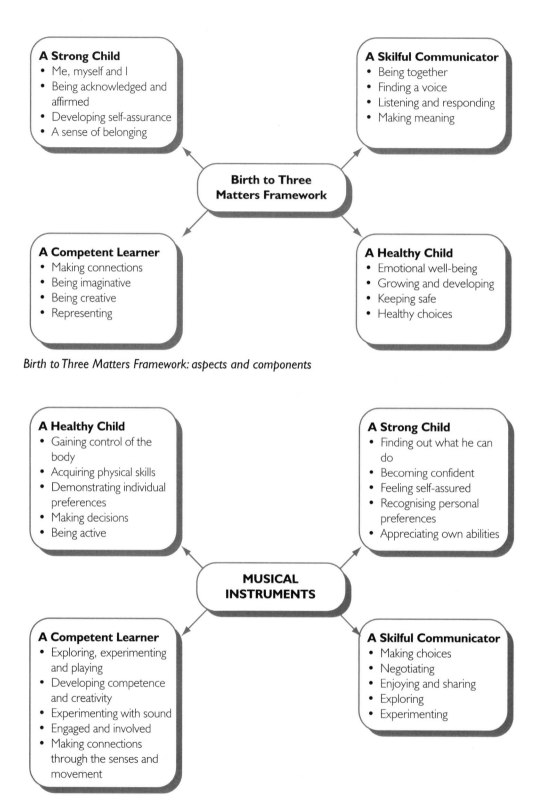

A Strong Child
- Me, myself and I
- Being acknowledged and affirmed
- Developing self-assurance
- A sense of belonging

A Skilful Communicator
- Being together
- Finding a voice
- Listening and responding
- Making meaning

Birth to Three Matters Framework

A Competent Learner
- Making connections
- Being imaginative
- Being creative
- Representing

A Healthy Child
- Emotional well-being
- Growing and developing
- Keeping safe
- Healthy choices

Birth to Three Matters Framework: aspects and components

A Healthy Child
- Gaining control of the body
- Acquiring physical skills
- Demonstrating individual preferences
- Making decisions
- Being active

A Strong Child
- Finding out what he can do
- Becoming confident
- Feeling self-assured
- Recognising personal preferences
- Appreciating own abilities

MUSICAL INSTRUMENTS

A Competent Learner
- Exploring, experimenting and playing
- Developing competence and creativity
- Experimenting with sound
- Engaged and involved
- Making connections through the senses and movement

A Skilful Communicator
- Making choices
- Negotiating
- Enjoying and sharing
- Exploring
- Experimenting

Birth to Three Matters Framework: how a music activity meets the aspects of the framework

Foundation Stage as a single quality framework for children aged 0–5. This will also include elements of the 14 National Standards in Childcare. These plans are based on the UK government's ten-year strategy for education. More information on this can be found at www.hm-treasury.gov.uk. The expected date for the finalisation of the Early Years Foundation Stage is 2008.

Other learning frameworks

Maria Montessori

Maria Montessori (1870–1952)

Maria Montessori was born in Italy on 31 August 1870. At a time when it was considered shocking for a woman to want to study medicine, and despite considerable opposition, including from her father, she succeeded in gaining a place at medical school. She graduated in 1896 as the first woman in Italy to do so.

During the course of her work for the University of Rome she became interested in the education of children with learning difficulties. In 1906 and 1907 she began working with 60 young children of working families and set up a 'Children's House' in San Lorenzo, one of the worst slum areas of Rome.

In this children's home, an environment was established where the children could develop their own activities. **Montessori** soon became aware that a child could easily absorb information from his or her own environment; she felt that the children were teaching themselves. She began to educate the older children on how to help out with everyday tasks using sense materials. She found that the children learnt very easily and the structure of the work gave the children a feeling of self-worth that they had not previously experienced. As a result of her work with the children, **Montessori** developed educational methods and materials which proved to be very successful.

The general attitude towards education at this time was very different to our views today. All children were given the same work to do at the same time, and were not seen as individuals with specific needs. Their capabilities were often under-estimated and they were not understood. In contrast **Montessori** set out to understand children and to work out how they learn about the world around them.

She realised that the children learnt a significant amount by using their senses and much of the equipment she devised took account of this. She designed exercises that would stimulate motor education, sensory education and language. The children were encouraged to participate in normal everyday activities, such as the preparation of the table for meals and the clearing away afterwards. There was a strong use of the outdoor environment and the furniture used was specifically designed to be lightweight so the children could arrange it themselves.

To improve the lives of the children she worked with in the slums, **Montessori** built relationships with their parents, encouraging them to realise their children were special.

Although **Maria Montessori** died in 1952 at the age of 82, the legacy of her work has continued and can be seen in Montessori schools throughout the world today and also in mainstream classrooms. In Montessori schools, it is possible to see an environment that uses **Montessori**'s educational philosophy and teaching methods, where the child is offered a unique and tailored education within a community of children, parents and teachers.

The basic concepts that **Montessori** developed ensured that:

- the teacher was guided by the child
- the child proceeded at his or her own pace
- imaginative teaching materials were used
- the materials were self-correcting so the child could see his or her own mistakes.

Impact on current practice

An early years practitioner walking into a Montessori school today would be interested to see the different equipment used by the children and to observe the role of the adults working with them. The learning materials are designed to develop each sense individually and are made from high-quality materials, often using fresh timber, such as beech, birch or maple wood. Everything in the Montessori classroom has a specific purpose and every piece of equipment is for the children to see, touch and use.

The adults are seen as facilitators of the children's learning. Montessori teachers are carefully trained to use the materials in a specific way in order to be able to teach the children appropriately. They must also learn to recognise when the child is ready to move on. Three stages of learning are involved:

1. The adult introduces the material to the child and teaches them how to use the equipment correctly.

2. The child processes the information received and develops an understanding of the concept through work and repetition.

3. The child demonstrates knowledge with ease and is able to teach someone else.

Montessori teachers are ideally highly trained through a specific course that reflects the philosophy of **Montessori** herself. The purpose of the trained teacher is to assist and direct (they are often termed 'directresses'), to stimulate the child's enthusiasm for learning and to guide it. They must not interfere with the child's natural desire to teach him/herself and become independent. Teachers in a Montessori school are expected to remain calm with the children, to move around the classroom in an unhurried and discreet manner and be responsive to the individual needs of the child. They must show the child respect and listen to the child's remarks and observations seriously.

Montessori schools tend not to use textbooks; the children generally learn directly from the environment or each other, rather than from the teacher. The teacher is trained to work with children on an individual basis, particularly as the children progress in independence or sometimes with a small group. The teacher will guide the child and conduct detailed observations that are carefully recorded. The observations record the level of concentration of each child, the way he or she responds to the equipment and his or her mastery of materials as well as social development and physical health. From these detailed observations the experienced teacher will be able to judge the stage a child is in and when the child is ready to progress.

Children learn from what they are doing as individuals but also from the richly varied environment around them. They are free to move around the room and to work on a piece of material with no time constraints. Many Montessori settings provide the children with individual trays or pieces of carpet where they can sit undisturbed on their own working with the materials. They will collect the material for themselves and return it to its correct place when they have finished. The children will often observe each other at work but they are encouraged not to interrupt or interfere with the other person.

Many Montessori settings arrange the environment according to subject areas. Within the age range of 3–6-year-olds, this often follows the areas of:

◆ practical life
◆ sensorial
◆ language
◆ maths
◆ cultural.

Other areas of the curriculum, such as botany and geography, history and timelines, will also be included and the children work to the same National Curriculum as other children aged 3–6, the Birth to Three Matters Framework and the Curriculum Guidance for the Foundation Stage.

How the subject areas in a Montessori school encourage development

	Development that is encouraged	Examples of materials
Practical life Reflects oneself, others and the environment.	◆ Co-ordination ◆ Independence ◆ Fine motor control ◆ Concentration ◆ Sense of order ◆ Ability to look after oneself An added purpose of practical life activities is that the real tasks involve the child's hands and mind working together which greatly increases the capacity to concentrate. This skill prepares the child for later intellectual work.	◆ Dressing frames that allow the child to practise dressing skills, such as learning how to tie bows and laces and do up zips, hooks and eyes and safety pins. ◆ Real-life activities such as pouring or spooning fluid from one container to another, setting out the cutlery for meals on low tables and washing up afterwards. ◆ Using scaled-down versions of real equipment, for example brushes and brooms, washing-up bowls, cleaning and polishing kits and even a tiny safe iron and ironing board.
Sensorial Gives children the opportunity to experience the physical properties of the world around them through using all their senses.	◆ Sense of order ◆ Discrimination and refinement of all five senses By carefully teaching children how to use the materials through active manipulation and leading them gradually, they will emerge as competent readers and writers.	◆ Rough and smooth boards ◆ Sound boxes containing sealed wooden cylinders that make a distinctive noise when shaken. ◆ Geometric cabinets containing geometric insets and frames containing shapes such as circles, rectangles, triangles. ◆ Sets of specially designed materials will be available to encourage the development of the senses, such as towers of blocks, fabrics to sort by touch, and puzzle blocks. The solid geometric blocks or solids are designed to be handled by small hands and have little knobs to hold between the finger and thumb, thus preparing the muscles of the hand for writing.

Language Recognises the vital importance of language to overall development.	◆ Letter sounds ◆ Reading ◆ Handwriting ◆ Grammar ◆ Vocabulary Writing often comes before reading in a Montessori setting as children build up their first words phonetically using cardboard letters. The reading programme progresses through three levels: pink, blue and green, and all reading materials are colour-coded to match the reading scheme.	◆ Lower case sandpaper letters ◆ Reading scheme and materials, for example a pink box containing a small dog. The child says the word 'dog' and then matches the letters to the sounds in the word. ◆ Wooden alphabet trays ◆ Insets for design to assist the development of pencil control – the children are given intricate shapes to colour and sandpaper letters are experienced by touch as well as sight and sound. ◆ Lots of picture and reference books are always available in the classroom.
Maths Activities enable children to learn mathematical concepts through the use of concrete materials.	◆ Number concepts ◆ Operations ◆ Time and money ◆ Measuring and fractions Children gain a physical impression of size and quantity before they begin to work with numbers through handling number rods, counting out beads, arranging colour counters in patterns of odd and even numbers. Sandpaper symbols are traced with their fingers so that number symbols are absorbed through touch as well as sight and sound.	◆ Numerical rods ◆ Sandpaper numbers ◆ Wooden number cards ◆ Wooden hundred board ◆ Golden beads

Cultural	Develops children's	Globes are provided, then study
Activities that teach children about the world beyond their immediate environment, recognising that young children are full of curiosity and are keen to explore.	awareness and knowledge of biology, geography, simple science and history.	◆ Globes are provided, then study maps using jigsaws. Children can trace and colour the shapes and fit them together as a puzzle. ◆ Picture cards of families and their daily lives and artefacts from other cultures, such as a Japanese fan or chopsticks and saris. ◆ The children celebrate festival days from different cultures by tasting foods, learning songs or talking to a visitor from that culture. ◆ Science materials might include magnets, lights and simple circuit boards. Most classrooms include a nature table or pets corner.

A typical day at a Montessori school may well follow a similar pattern to a mainstream early years setting with children being welcomed individually to the session and having the opportunity to interact freely with the environment and explore the materials available. However, the session is organised in a 'work cycle' which enables children to work individually on self-chosen activities which reflect the interwoven approach of integrated studies. Classes often comprise children of different ages which enables them to learn from each other, closely monitored by the adult. As children are so involved in the learning process, it is often possible to have quite large groups of children present at any session.

> ### Key aspects of a Montessori School for 3–6-year-olds
> ◆ Highly structured materials with a particular way to use them
> ◆ Objects made from natural materials
> ◆ Four key areas of learning – practical life, sensorial, language and maths
> ◆ The adults are led by the children and guide them
> ◆ Close monitoring through observations by the adults
> ◆ Children very involved in the learning process
> ◆ Children encouraged to learn from each other
> ◆ Importance to the child of the environment as a learning tool

Many children educated in a Montessori pre-school will later attend mainstream school and it is the aim that the children will be able to transfer their skills of independent learning, involvement in their activities and a curious mind to their new environment.

One criticism that has been levelled at the Montessori approach to education is that it does not reflect fantasy and the use of the imagination in its curriculum. Traditionally, in a Montessori setting there are no areas for role play commonly seen in a mainstream early years settings, such as the home corner. However, **Maria Montessori** saw imagination and creativity as important aspects of the developing child and the child's experience. Art, dance, music and drama are integrated into the curriculum and imagination is seen to play a crucial role as children interact with the natural world.

Montessori is also discussed in Chapter 6, page 175.

Rudolf Steiner

Dr **Rudolf Steiner** was born in Kraljevec, in what is now Croatia. He spent his childhood and teenage years in the vicinity of Vienna and from the age of 18 studied maths, physics, chemistry and natural history at the Technical University there. His illustrious and highly respected academic career started with the publication, at the age of 21, of the natural scientific works of Goethe, a central figure in nineteenth-century German culture.

Rudolf Steiner (1861–1925)

Throughout his life, **Steiner** was seen as a great thinker and philosopher with a scientist's interest in the natural and man-made world. He inspired innovation through the wide-ranging areas of education, medicine, social development and art. His ideas inspired people to create a movement known as 'anthroposophy' which embraces the study of spiritual science, eurhythmy and nature. Eurhythmy can be described as beautiful or harmonious movement. The anthroposophy movement is still in evidence today with the headquarters in Switzerland and members in the USA.

Through education, **Steiner** wanted to give children the opportunity to develop clarity of thought, sensitivity of feeling and strength of will. He saw education as being an art that was creative and individual and led children to spiritual awareness through educating the whole child. There was a strong emphasis on balancing the child's natural stages of development with creativity and academic excellence, through the arts, social skills and spiritual values.

At the end of the Second World War, when Europe was in a chaotic state, **Steiner** was asked to develop a school for the workers at the Waldorf Astoria cigarette factory in Stuttgart. The director of the factory, Emil Molt, wanted a school for his workers that incorporated an innovative approach to education, based upon **Steiner**'s ideas, where children of wealthy families could also be educated. At the opening of this school, **Steiner** insisted that the school be open to all children and that it should be run by the teachers without interference from the state.

Impact on current practice

The approach pioneered in Stuttgart became the foundation for the worldwide Steiner Waldorf schools found around the world today. There are more than 900 schools and 1800 kindergartens in more than 60 countries worldwide. Some of the kindergartens are attached to Steiner Waldorf schools, while others are independent. The curriculum is based upon **Steiner**'s view that the education of the whole child needed to reflect the importance of educating the development of the child, morally, spiritually, physically and academically, and was based on three integrated levels of development:

◆ the head, or the intellect – teaching the child to think for him or herself

◆ the heart – instilling a sense of feeling and spirit

◆ the hands – involvement of the arts and crafts.

Steiner schools work hard to create a strong feeling of community between the pupils, teachers, staff, parents and old pupils.

Steiner developed a model of child development that is used in the schools today, based upon three stages:

◆ kindergarten (early years to age 7)

◆ middle school (7–14 years)

◆ upper school (14–19 years).

These stages are described in the table below.

Steiner's model of schooling

Stage	Description of the stage
Kindergarten – from birth until approximately 7 years	The child learns through imitation and example so needs to be surrounded by caring adults and the good things about the world. An emphasis is placed on activities that reflect traditional household tasks such as cooking and helping with chores. Children are not taught academic subjects such as reading and writing but they are exposed to story-telling, rhymes, movement and music, with a strong emphasis on the use of their individual imagination.
Middle school – 7–14 years	Children are deemed ready for this stage when the initial stage of physical growth has finished. An example of this is when the teeth begin to change. During this stage, academic activities are integrated with the arts through spiritual, physical and craft activities. This stage is designed to be challenging, structured and creative. In many schools, the teacher will stay with the class throughout the entire stage if possible.
Upper school – 14–19 years	The child is guided by teachers to become independent in thought, to discover his own understanding of worldwide issues and make his own judgements. At this stage, the child will receive guidance from a number of specialist teachers rather than just one.

An overall impression on walking into a Steiner kindergarten today is one of calmness, with the children involved in purposeful activity. The play equipment is stored within the children's reach with a predominance of natural materials and soft, warm colours. Typical equipment might include wooden tables, planks and stools, plain coloured cloths, baskets of natural materials such as shells, logs, pebbles, and soft dolls made of material to cuddle and dress. Ideally there will be lots of space for the children to carry out their imaginative games and to make dens and houses from the softly draped materials. The adults at the kindergarten will also carry out tasks which the children can join in with, such as baking bread, making soup, weaving or cleaning. Staff will encourage the children to join in activities such as tidying up after a morning of playing by singing a 'tidying-up' song and by starting to put the equipment away in its chosen place. The age range of children within the kindergarten often leads to the older children teaching and encouraging the younger children.

Teachers will lead a part of the session called 'ring time' through finger rhymes and traditional stories and poems. This particular part of the session is often linked to the changing seasons of the year. Snacks provided for the children, and which they participate in preparing, are organic in nature and based on grain such as apple crumble, soup and vegetables and bread.

As with the Montessori approach to education, the adult has a particular role to play. When the children arrive at the kindergarten, for example, the adults will already be involved in work-based activities. These tasks are suitable for the children to join in with and often follow a rhythm that flows throughout the week with activities such as cooking, baking, cleaning taking place on regular days of the week so that the children know what to expect. This follows a general belief that children need to feel secure and know what to expect. During the session there is opportunity for a quiet time that encourages reverence. **Steiner** believed that there was also a need for repetition throughout the day to establish continuity and aid the development of the memory. Stories are often repeated many times and daily, weekly and yearly events are anticipated.

The children will create the games that they play and the adult role is to be on hand, reminding the children through song to use small voices within the indoor environment. The teacher will also observe the children whilst she is engaged in an activity herself and may invite a child to join her if they are having particular difficulties with the social play.

Adults will also provide opportunity for outdoor play and in most kindergartens this will be provided every day, regardless of the weather. Ideally there will be provision on-site for gardening and woodwork, as well as playing outdoors, and the adult will continue to be engaged in tasks that need to be done, such as leaf sweeping, that are appropriate for each season of the year. As with the indoor setting, the children will join in with the tasks and the older children will help the younger ones.

Story time is seen as a quiet activity and the traditionally told stories, usually known off by heart by the adult, are designed to stimulate the imagination of the children who can create pictures in their own minds. A mood of dreaminess is created by the use of candles and the telling of the story over several days.

Key aspects of a Steiner kindergarten

◆ Calm approach to the children

◆ Rhythm, repetition and reverence within the week's activities

◆ Emphasis on play and domestic work

◆ Wide range of children's ages and an emphasis on the younger children being helped by the older children

◆ Natural materials used within the setting

◆ Importance of outdoor play recognised

◆ Provision of organic food

◆ Strong emphasis on the use of the child's imagination

Teachers working in a Steiner kindergarten will work closely with parents by sharing their experiences and observations of the children and in explaining the ethos and beliefs of the Steiner approach. Some families will start their children by attending parent and child groups before the child starts at the kindergarten, and this is an opportunity for them to really understand this approach to early years education.

TRY IT OUT

You may have the opportunity to visit a Steiner kindergarten and take part in a session. While you observe the rhythm of the session, try to absorb the philosophy behind the activities that you see. Look carefully at the involvement of the children and the role of the staff.

At the end of the session, take the opportunity to talk to the staff and compare their views with your own. Consider the following points:

- ◆ *What was the ethos of the setting?*
- ◆ *What have you seen that is very different to the approach in your setting?*
- ◆ *What can you take back and use in your own practice?*
- ◆ *How does this approach differ to the Montessori school?*
- ◆ *What opportunities do the children you work with have for imaginative play? What else could you provide that would encourage imaginative play?*

One of the key differences that you may notice between the Montessori school and the Steiner approach is the different types of equipment available and the way that this equipment is used. The role of the adult is also fundamentally different in their approach to the structure of the day, with the Steiner teacher involved in her own tasks which the child is encouraged to join in and help with. The Montessori teacher has particular tasks to teach the child initially in a highly structured way before they practise these for themselves. There is a less obvious emphasis on imaginative play, although creativity and imagination are acknowledged as important learning tools.

The Steiner approach does allow children to learn in this way throughout their school lives by attending the school from kindergarten through to upper school. The foundations established in the kindergarten are built upon in the lower school and similarly from the lower to upper school. The three levels of education are often on the same site, enabling a sense of community to develop. Some children leave the Steiner approach at the kindergarten stage and attend mainstream schools where they are able to use the skills they have learnt of using their imagination and having social confidence and an enthusiasm for learning. Children who start mainstream education at 6 years old will need to undertake the formal skills of reading and writing which have not been addressed in the kindergarten.

THINK ABOUT IT

Reflect on the following and discuss with colleagues.

Steiner felt that children who were forced into formal education too early and pressured to succeed intellectually lacked the motivation to learn for themselves. He also felt it was very important to foster the child's personal and social development through play and the use of the imagination. He felt this encouraged the child to concentrate and learn to be inventive and adaptable.

◆ Do you think that children need to develop their imagination?

◆ In your opinion, are there dangers to introducing the child to formal education at an early age? If so, what are they?

◆ Is it possible to be put off learning? Reflect on your own experiences.

◆ How can we ensure that children leave our setting wanting to learn?.

The Reggio Emilia approach to early years education

Reggio Emilia is a small town in northern Italy that has become internationally famous for its approach to early years education. It is so well known that people from all over the world visit the town to observe the work that is going on there. An exhibition, 'The 100 Languages of Children', tours the world showing some of the amazing work completed by the young children with their teachers.

The story of how the Reggio Emilia approach began is simple. In the aftermath of the Second World War, when Italy lay in ruins and poverty was commonplace, a small amount of money was raised by the people of Reggio Emilia from the sale of a piece of military equipment left behind in the town. The community decided, after much discussion, that they wanted to invest it in education in order to create a better society for their children to grow up in. They occupied a disused building and turned it into a nursery school, following it later by other nursery schools built by the people of the town. The effort and will of the people was guided by a young and inspirational teacher, Loris Malaguzzi, who dedicated his life to the development of the philosophy behind the Reggio approach. Loris Malaguzzi was influenced by the views of Vygotsky, Piaget and Bruner (see pages 42–67) in that he promoted the idea of children as active participators in their own learning in a unique reciprocal relationship with their teacher. There was also a strong belief in the importance of the community and of the use of the expressive arts as a vehicle for learning.

There are currently 13 infant-toddler centres for children aged from infancy to 3 years and 21 pre-schools for the 3–6-year-olds in Reggio Emilia. The environment within which the children work is seen as very important, sometimes referred to as the third educator, after the parents and teachers, and reflects the developmental needs of young children. Within each of the settings there is a piazza, a central meeting place where the children can gather and play and chat together. A typical piece of equipment found here is a tetrahedron made of mirrors which the children can crawl inside. This is an amazing experience for anyone lucky enough to climb inside one, whether child or adult, as the experience allows you to see an infinite amount of yourself from every angle. It stimulates thought and conversation and endless possibility, as every time you change position you see a different perspective of yourself and your friends.

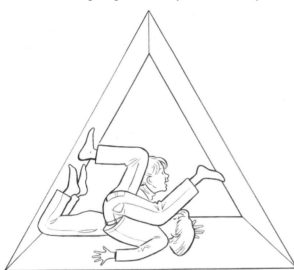

The Reggio Emilia tetrahedron

The buildings reflect light and space with a series of connecting spaces that flow into one another where the child can move freely. The philosophy behind this is to encourage the children to participate and interact with each other, and it reflects the differences that the children, teachers and community bring to the whole experience. The environment is designed to be flexible and to evolve as the year progresses, so the furniture is multi-functional and screens are used to divide the space in different ways. The equipment is accessible for the children and stored in see-through containers so that children can find things easily. Mirrors are used extensively to enable the child to understand him or herself in relation to the environment. Multi-sensory activities encourage the children to look at colour and textures in a stimulating way. The colour in the buildings is provided by the children themselves through their artwork and clothing.

In the pre-schools, there is also an art studio (an atelier) where children work with an experienced and qualified artist (an atelierista) who is also a member of staff. The importance of the use of the expressive arts is fundamental to the Reggio approach because it is acknowledged that:

◆ children of a young age are very expressive and have an enormous capacity for showing their feelings and emotions and of using their imaginations

◆ the learning process is more important than the end product. Children can revisit subjects that interest them over and over again through expressive arts

◆ children's ability to express themselves through non-verbal languages may be devalued if too much emphasis is put on the development of their verbal and literacy skills. The staff place a lot of value on the use of non-verbal communication such as painting, music, sculpture, dance and drawing

◆ children can use the expressive arts to look at and experience the world in many different ways such as observation or by making pictures that represent smells or noises.

Source: Adapted from Valentine (1999)

During the course of a day at the pre-school, children are given the opportunity to do detailed drawings or to participate in a variety of activities such as sculpture, shadow play, puppetry, painting, dancing, music, ceramics, writing and construction. The standard of work that the children achieve is internationally recognised and no one visiting Reggio Emilia or the 100 languages exhibition can fail to be astounded at the creativity, energy and skill demonstrated.

The children's work does not go home at the end of the day, but is discussed and documented. An early year's adviser, the pedagogista, works with the schools to reflect on the learning and then will take work to the common Documentation Centre where the work is published on large boards to empower and support all the teachers of the community.

Loris Malaguzzi talked about the child having a hundred languages and more. The child is seen as being rich in potential, strong, powerful and eager to interact and contribute to the world. The poem below demonstrates how important the child is to the educators of Reggio Emilia and the sense of the young child as having infinite potential that can be easily taken away if handled without care.

NO WAY – THE HUNDRED IS THERE

The child
is made of one hundred.

The child has
a hundred languages
a hundred hands
a hundred thoughts
a hundred ways of thinking
of playing, of speaking.

A hundred, always a hundred
ways of listening
of marveling, of loving,
a hundred joys
for singing and understanding

a hundred worlds
to discover
a hundred worlds
to invent
a hundred worlds
to dream.
The child has
a hundred languages
(and a hundred hundred hundred more)
but they steal ninety-nine.

The school and the culture
separate the head from the body.
They tell the child
to think without hands
to do without head
to listen and not to speak
to understand without joy
to love and to marvel
only at Easter and Christmas.
They tell the child
to discover the world already there
and of the hundred
they steal ninety-nine.
They tell the child
that work and play
reality and fantasy
science and imagination
sky and earth
reason and dream
are things
that do not belong together.

And thus they tell the child
that the hundred is not there.
The child says
'No way – The hundred is there.'

by Loris Malaguzzi (Gandini, 1996)

Role of the teachers

The adults working as teachers are trained from the age of 14 and spend five years studying formally. During this time, they are taught how to listen to children, to observe, to respect and learn from children. They are also taught how to act as researchers based upon observations. After the completion of the formal period of training, teachers continue with professional development throughout the course of each day and they are seen as learners in their own right. All the teachers are given non-contact time to give them time to talk together about the children and to be able to write up their observations and plan what will be offered to the children next. The observations allow teachers to understand what interests the child and how to plan suitable topics to encourage development. Knowledge of the children will also be established through interaction with the parents and community.

The projects that the children work through are based on this understanding of the children and on the teacher's knowledge of topics that naturally interest children. They do not follow rigid timetables but meander gently along at the child's own pace. Some of the projects take months to complete, depending on the interest and involvement of the children. Children often return to a topic or piece of work some time after their initial interest has passed and are asked to revisit and show how they would complete the work now they are older. This encourages the child to reflect and to see how they have progressed. Children are also encouraged to develop projects and solve problems themselves, using the teacher as a 'tool' to help them. A reciprocal relationship of love and trust is encouraged between the child and the teacher and between the children.

The role of the teacher is to:

◆ understand the child as an individual

◆ build a mutually trusting relationship with the child

◆ support and encourage the child on the learning journey

◆ challenge or provoke ideas through open-ended questioning

◆ respect the child's own ideas

◆ allow the child to make his own mistakes and learn from them

◆ closely observe the children to judge appropriate moments to intervene

◆ remain with the child for a three-year period

- observe the learning process and document carefully using a variety of means, such as audio, video, photographs and written notes
- share and discuss documentation with colleagues.

CASE STUDY:

JOURNEY TO THE OUTER REACHES OF THE LIVING

The children sent a letter to Santa Claus asking for a big tank for fish. When the tank arrived, it proved to be a spark for a lengthy topic. The children began to fill the tank, even before it was set up, with suggestions for it to hold whales, swordfish, sharks, seals and crocodiles. In reality, the children filled the tank with frogs, toads, and other small animals found in the local canals and rivers.

The children carried out detailed observational drawings of the creatures and decided that they wanted to create a bigger living space for them. They decided to build a pond with the help of their parents. The adults accepted the challenge and one Sunday a group of fathers dug a hole in the school yard. Over the next few months the pond was completed. The provision of the pond enabled the children to study even more exciting creatures and over the next three years the tank and the pond enabled them to travel to the outer reaches of the living.

Source: Gandini (1996), page 188

Teachers also work closely with the parents and community to share the education of the child and the nurturing of parent–school relationships is a key element of the Reggio approach. This encourages continuity in the child's life and ensures the community is an integral part of the school. Parents and the community run the schools through elected membership of the school's council and through active involvement in the upkeep of the school and participation in celebrations and outings. Meetings are held with the family before the child starts at the school to enable the teachers to build an image of the child. The schools also play a role in adult learning through the provision of practical sessions and talks where parents can discuss issues related to the care and education of their children.

Impact on current practice

The Reggio Emilia approach is unique in the way that it draws a whole community together to work for the education of the young child in such a significant way. It would not be possible to replicate this in its entirety in the UK today, but there is much that can be learnt from this approach and used to enhance the learning taking place in early years settings. It is useful to understand some of the key features and to reflect on our provision and approach.

> **Key features of the Reggio Emilia approach**
>
> ◆ The environment as an educator
>
> ◆ The importance of observing children and documenting their progress
>
> ◆ Partnerships with parents and the wider community
>
> ◆ The role of the adult
>
> ◆ Professional development
>
> ◆ Valuing and encouraging child-initiated activity
>
> ◆ Teachers have the time to reflect and discuss practice and children with colleagues
>
> ◆ The importance of the expressive arts

THINK ABOUT IT

Consider the key features of the Reggio Emilia approach to learning listed above. Discuss with colleagues how they could be used to enhance the work you do.

You may have considered the ideas in the table below.

How the key features of the Reggio Emilia approach could enhance provision

Key features of the Reggio Emilia approach	How it can be used to enhance our own provision
The environment as an educator	The environment could be structured in such a way to encourage children to be active in their learning. Materials could be easily accessible and an area could be established where children of different ages can meet and talk about ideas. A variety of stimuli could be provided to encourage children to problem solve and be creative in their learning. Space could be given for children to create their own environments.
The importance of observing children and documenting their progress	Adults can discuss how to observe the children in ways that increases their understanding of the children and their interests. Imaginative ways of documenting and displaying progress could be considered

Partnership with parents and the wider community	Consideration can be given to how the parents are viewed in the setting and how they are actively involved in their children's education. Are they valued as their child's first educator? How is the community involved with the setting? Are there opportunities for inclusion at meetings and talks about child development and education? Is the setting used for adult learning as well?
The role of the adult	Adults can think about their role in empowering children as learners and how to build a relationship based on mutual trust. Consideration can be given to how to listen to children's ideas and opinions.
Professional development	Professional development to be included in day-to-day practice and time given to adults to discuss their understanding of the children.
Valuing and encouraging child-initiated activity	The adults can give the children the opportunity to make mistakes and learn from them by intervening less in their play. Adults can consider how to encourage children to make decisions and plan activities and to flow with ideas that spark their interest.
Having time to reflect and discuss practice and children with colleagues	Time can be allocated for adults to reflect on their practice and the children's experiences.
The importance of the expressive arts	The importance of creativity can be discussed and ways to include the expressive arts within the provision.

An important aspect of the educators in the Reggio Emilia approach is the development of reflective practice. This is a way of thinking about our practice and not becoming complacent about the experiences offered to children. The following questions will encourage you to reflect on the purpose of the provision you are offering children.

THINK ABOUT IT

Reflect on these key questions posed by Carlina Rinaldi at a lecture in 1999:

- What do we hope for our children?
- What do we expect from children?
- What is the relationship between school, family and society?.

Forest Schools

The idea of the Forest School originated in Sweden in the 1950s when a retired soldier started teaching children about their environment through songs and stories and practical experiences in the woods and forests. The idea of the Forest School was adopted by the Danish and soon became an integral part of the early years programme of education.

Such schools are now found in the UK with the first one sited at Bridgewater College in Somerset in 1995 where it is linked to the Nursery and Early Years Centre of Excellence. It arose from a visit by college lecturers to a school in Denmark where they had seen young children using and exploring their outdoor environment. The benefits to the children were numerous and the lecturers resolved to create a similar setting in England. The beginnings were small, with the children initially taken to the college sports field and taught how to respect their environment and to work in teams. They were shown how to use tools such as saws and axes which needed careful planning and high adult:child ratios. By the end of the first year, the project had been so successful that it was expanded by hiring a minibus and an area of woodland for the children to use. The 3 and 4-year-old children were taken to the forest accompanied by qualified staff and second year students. The children used their new environment to explore and build their knowledge of their forest through practical activities.

Children having fun at a Forest School

Forest Schools in general hold the belief that children of all ages and abilities can benefit from the education available through the outdoors environment. Children as young as 3 years are encouraged to take part and the activities are planned for their individual needs. The outdoors is used in a deliberate and structured way to teach children practical and social skills. The children are set small and manageable tasks that they can succeed at and given genuine praise for their efforts; nobody is set up to fail. This encourages confidence, enthusiasm and further involvement by the child and forms a basis for all future learning. Many children who have previously found structured activities or school environments difficult to cope with, and have subsequently showed challenging behaviour, have shown marked progress at the Forest School.

THINK ABOUT IT

◆ Can you remember a time when, as a child, you were able to run and play in the woods or a forest? How did it feel?

◆ Have you taken children to a forest? How did they react? Did they enjoy it?

◆ What do you think are the benefits of learning outdoors?

You may have remembered your own experiences of playing in forests with enthusiasm and pleasure and you may have recalled a sense of freedom from running through the leaves and bracken and a sense of power and achievement from climbing the trees. You may also have remembered some of the imaginative games that you played – of pirates in the crow's nest or Robin Hood saving Maid Marian from the Sheriff of Nottingham. There is also the sense of smallness that the tall trees induce and the terror of being discovered when playing hide and seek.

There are benefits of working in the outdoor environment in this way:

◆ Children have the opportunity to practise their developing skills, particularly in physical development.

◆ Modern children are exhibiting higher levels of obesity and potential heart problems than ever before. They need regular vigorous physical activity.

◆ It provides opportunity for safe outdoor play which many children are denied.

◆ The children feel good about their achievements.

◆ It can increase self-confidence and assurance, team working skills and levels of concentration.

◆ Children have the opportunity to feel what it is like to be out in the fresh air, using tools.

◆ Children have the opportunity to make choices and decisions for themselves.

◆ Even young children can feel what it is like to be alone in a safe environment.

◆ Children acquire a deeper understanding of environmental issues.

◆ Children who have previously found learning difficult will achieve success and be motivated to try more challenging activities.

◆ It is fun and increases a sense of well-being.

At Forest Schools, the children are given the freedom to explore and take part in challenging activities that include an element of controlled danger. This provides the child with a fun experience and the opportunity to lead the activities which enhances self-confidence and self-esteem.

Impact on current practice

There are now several Forest Schools around the UK and many other initiatives to encourage children and adults to use the outdoor environment for learning.

CASE STUDY:

FOREST EDUCATION INITIATIVE

In Hertfordshire, the Groundwork Hertfordshire team is working with London North East and Herts cluster groups on the Magic Wood Project. This is an environmental education project focusing on the subject of 'wood as a resource' for learning. Workshops will be delivered in five Hertfordshire schools to primary age children which will look at the importance of wood as a resource and the woodland eco-system. It will include tree-planting sessions and visits to woodlands at Hatfield House and Harebreaks Woodland. There will also be a trip to the Apsley Paper Trail where the children will be shown how to make paper and to the Countryside Management Service to learn how and why trees are coppiced.

Source: www.foresteducation.org

It is generally felt that, if children are to experience maximum benefit from Forest Schools, they need to be attending them regularly, ideally on a weekly basis throughout the year. This way the child is able to appreciate the changes in the forest through all seasons and weathers and can participate in activities that are season-related, such as making bonfires, coppicing, observing bluebells and wood anemones. Many of the activities, for instance lighting fires and chopping wood, would normally be prohibited, but during the first part of the school year the children learn the safety rules for the forest. The activities are carefully and gradually developed so that the build up to more dangerous activities is very gradual. For example, children learn about approaching a camp fire long before they have a chance to light it.

The safety of the children is paramount so the adult:child ratio is very high, often 1:4 with leaders supernumerary. The Forest will be secure, often in the middle of fields and surrounded by fences. Forest School leaders are trained in techniques that enable the children to experience fire-lighting, building shelters and bridges, using penknives, saws, ropes and maps or producing artwork that uses the natural materials available in the forest. Activities undertaken at the Forest School will often be discussed and shared, and links are made to the Foundation Stage Curriculum to enable the children to meet the early learning goals.

The table below outlines other important influences on the use of the outdoor environment and supports the work of the Forest Schools.

Important influences on the use of the outdoor environment

Friedrich Froebel	Recognised the importance of the outside environment in educating young children and talked about the use of the garden for helping young children to learn.
Margaret McMillan	Spoke about the importance of children's health to their overall well-being and created a nursery at Deptford where the children could use the large garden to play and exercise. She also established a large, residential camp in Kent so that London children could experience the countryside.
Susan Isaacs	Encouraged children to use the outdoor environment to explore and find out about their environment.
Chelsea Open-Air Nursery School	Founded by an American in 1929, it encouraged children of rich families in Chelsea to face physical challenges and take risks.
Woodcraft Folk	An organisation that promotes activities for children and young people to give them a deeper understanding of environmental issues with a key focus on sustainable development. Founded in Britain in the New Forest in 1925, it is based on the work of Ernest Thompson Seton, a naturalist and writer in North America, who allowed local children to play in his garden and taught them Native American folklore and craft. Groups meet weekly and the programme includes regular weekends away, camping and opportunities to visit other groups abroad. Children are taught to have respect and an appreciation for nature and to co-operate with each other.
Curriculum Guidance for the Foundation Stage	This guidance refers to the need for teachers to provide the opportunity for children to have access to regular and frequent physical activity indoors and outdoors, with the possibility of spontaneous movement between the two environments. The use of natural materials, such as a fallen tree or a pile of leaves, is mentioned as an inexpensive resource that involves all the senses, providing they are safe to use. (Curriculum Guidance for the Foundation Stage, pages 101 and 102)

Froebel, McMillan and Isaacs are discussed in Chapter 6, pages 168, 176 and 173.

THINK ABOUT IT

Consider the outdoor provision available at your setting.

◆ What are the learning opportunities for the children?

◆ Do you use the environment effectively?

◆ Could you incorporate any of the ideas of the Forest Schools in your setting, for example providing the children with challenges within a safe environment?

◆ How can you encourage the children to explore their environment and be more aware of the changing seasons?

◆ Could you establish links with a local wooded area where the children could visit regularly?

Summary

This chapter has considered the curriculum frameworks used by early years settings to structure the learning of children in their care. This has included the legislative frameworks of the Curriculum Guidance for the Foundation Stage and the Birth to Three Matters Framework for the younger children. We have found that both of these clearly state the expectations for appropriate activities and experiences that promote and extend development with clear guidance for practitioners. The principles underpinning the frameworks have been discussed and we considered the impact of these on professional practice. You have been encouraged to reflect upon your own practice in relation to these principles.

We have also looked at other influential and relevant frameworks based upon the ideas and philosophies of **Maria Montessori** and **Rudolf Steiner** and discussed how these are interpreted and used today.

The exciting developments in educational practice of the Reggio Emilia approach and the Forest Schools has also been discussed and you have been encouraged to think about the elements of these that can be adapted and used in your own setting.

Throughout the chapter we have endeavoured to assist you in considering the elements of a framework that promote quality practice and provide children with the best possible start to their educational life.

CHECK YOUR UNDERSTANDING

1 What do you consider are the key features of the Curriculum Guidance for the Foundation Stage?

2 How would you describe the philosophy of the Waldorf-Steiner schools?

3 What are the differences between the approach of a Montessori nursery and a mainstream setting?

4 What are the aims of the Forest Schools?

5 What influence has the Reggio Emilia approach had on current work in schools?

References and further reading

Abbott, L. and Nutbrown, C. (eds) (2001) *Experiencing Reggio Emilia: Implications for pre-school provision*, Open University Press

DfES (2000) *Curriculum Guidance for the Foundation Stage*, QCA (QCA Orderline, PO Box 29, Norwich NR3 1GN, 08700 606015, ref. QCA/00/587; www.qca.org.uk/160.html)

DfES/Sure Start (2002) *Birth to Three Matters: A framework to support children in their earliest years*, DfES (DfES Publications Centre, PO Box 5050, Annesley, Nottingham NG15 0DJ,0845 022260; or download from www.standards.dfes.gov.uk/primary/publications/foundation_stage/9400463)

Fidler, W. (2006) 8-page supplement, *EYE Magazine*, January; www.intered.uk.com

Gandini, L. (trans) (1996) *The Hundred Languages of Children*, exhibition catalogue, Reggio Children, Unipol Assicurazioni

Kingman, S. (2003) 'Good practice: the magic of Reggio', *Practical Pre-School*, Issue 42, December

Kramer, R. (1976) *Maria Montessori*, G.P. Putman

Pound, L. (2005) *How Children Learn*, Step Forward Publishing

Rinaldi, C. (1999) 'The Image of the Child', Reggio Children British Study Tour, April

Taplin, J. (2006) 8-page supplement, *EYE Magazine*, February

Valentine, M. (1999) *The Reggio Emilia Approach to Early Years Education*, Scottish Consultative Council on the Curriculum

Useful websites

www.webster.edu/~woolflm/montessori2.html – information on **Maria Montessori**

www.montessori-uk.org – official website giving information about **Maria Montessori**'s life and philosophy, links to other websites, information about training, publications and schools

www.steinerwaldorf.org.uk – information about the philosophy of **Rudolf Steiner**, publications available including videos, the nature of educational establishments and training available

www.steinerbooks.org/aboutrudolf.html – books by **Rudolf Steiner** to purchase

www.ltl.org.uk – information about Landscapes for Learning

www.foresteducation.org.uk – information about education through woodlands and forests across the UK

www.bridgwater.ac.uk – Bridgwater College

www.woodcraft.org.uk – Woodcraft Folk

www.surestart.gov.uk – information about the Birth to Three Matters Framework

www.standards.dfes.gov.uk – to download the Birth to Three Matters Framework

Chapter 2

How children learn

Introduction

As an early years practitioner, you need to understand how children learn in order to provide appropriate activities and experiences that encourage progress. There are many different opinions about how children develop intellectually, and you will soon discover that it is not always easy to understand the theory and then put it into practice. However, many theorists have been influential in determining how we work with children on a day-to-day basis and it is important for practitioners to be aware of this in order to provide high-quality care and education.

In the twenty-first century, we are privileged to have a wealth of knowledge about children and how they develop and learn. This knowledge is continually being revised and updated through systematic professional research.

In this chapter, we will consider the work of selected theorists and researchers and the implications for practice. These theorists have been chosen for their continuing influence on early years practice and for the significant impact their work has had on our understanding of how children learn and for their inspiration to educators and others. We will also look at your role in promoting learning.

This chapter covers:

◆ The work of theorists and researchers on how children learn
◆ The role of the early years practitioner in promoting learning.

The theorists and researchers covered in this chapter are:

◆ **Jean Piaget**, page 42
◆ **Tina Bruce**, page 52
◆ **Lev Vygotsky**, page 58
◆ **Jerome Bruner**, page 62.

Work of theorists and researchers on how children learn

Jean Piaget

Jean Piaget (1896–1980)

Jean Piaget spent over 60 years observing children through naturally occurring research, mainly using his own children. His contribution to our knowledge of child development is phenomenal and forms the basis of much of the work that is carried out currently in early years settings.

Primarily a biologist and philosopher, **Piaget** was interested in the way that children think and how they viewed the world. His work led him to believe that children develop in stages and that they must progress through these stages in chronological order. **Piaget** has been very influential in determining the current practice of providing developmentally-appropriate activities.

Piaget maintained that there were four stages of cognitive development through which a child passed before reaching adulthood:

1 Sensori-motor – birth to 2 years

2 Pre-operational – 2–7 years

3 Concrete operations – 7–11/12 years

4 Formal operations – 11/12–16 years.

The key features of each stage are outlined in the table on pages 44–46.

Piaget devised tests to gauge the level of thought the child had reached. These tests included:

◆ *decentring*: the child was provided with a three-dimensional model of mountains and figures, and asked to describe what each figure could see. If the child was unable to do so, Piaget deemed that the child was egocentric and therefore unable to see someone else's point of view.

◆ *conservation of number*: counters were set out in identical rows. The child was asked to agree that the rows were identical in number. The position of the counters in one of the rows was then changed in front of the child. If the child had understanding of conservation, he or she would realise that the number of counters remained the same although the appearance of the rows had changed. A child who was unable to conserve would consider that the longer row had more counters in it. Similar tests were devised to test conservation of volume and mass.

Using the conservation test

Conservation of number

1   Place two identical rows of ten counters in front of the child.

2   Ask them: 'Does each row have the same number of counters?' The child may wish to count them.

3   If the child agrees that each row has the same amount, change the appearance of one of the rows by making the gap between the counters larger. This must be done in front of the child. The rows will now look visibly different.

4   Ask the child again: 'Does each row have the same number of counters?'

5   If the child understands that the rows still have the same number, despite the change in appearance, they have understood that things stay the same even if the appearance changes.

Conservation of mass

Carry out the same test as for number, but this time use two equally sized balls of play dough. Make sure the child agrees that the balls are the same size, and then change the shape of one ball to a sausage shape. Will the child understand that the amount of dough has stayed the same even though the appearance has changed?

Conservation of volume

Carry out the same test as for number, but this time use transparent containers of water that are the same. To change the appearances pour one of the containers of water into a different shaped container. Will the child understand that the amount of water has stayed the same even though the appearance has changed?

A child involved in Piaget's test for conservation

Choose a group of children within the 4–7 years age range who will be happy to answer some questions. Try carrying out a conservation test with individual children in a quiet part of the room.

By using these tests you will recognise that children may not see things in the same way as adults do. This means that planned activities should consider the level of understanding a child has reached.

How do practitioners use Piaget's theory of learning?

As a practitioner, you will be aware of the numerous activities and experiences that young children are exposed to during the time that they are in your setting and the routine that a typical day follows. You may not be as aware of the reasons why certain activities are included and the theory that provides the basis for the work that is going on. A close study of **Piaget**'s work begins to reveal how his theories have been influential in current early years practice.

The influence of Piaget on current early years practice

Stage of development	Key features	Links to early years practice
Sensori-motor 0–2 years	The child's early development is dependent on their ability to use their senses. Information about the world around them will come from the sights, sounds, tastes, smells and touch that they experience. As the child starts to move, there are more opportunities for him to use his senses to absorb information. In the first few weeks of life, a baby is mainly learning through reflexes but later the baby begins to repeat actions and then to interact with objects, seeing what they can do. At this stage, the child needs the opportunity to explore. As the concept of object permanence develops (the understanding that an object still exists even if it can't be seen), the child is able to manipulate objects more and find out about their properties and uses. Gradually words will develop to categorise objects.	◆ Provision of sensory experiences, for example treasure baskets, music, mobiles, different textured foods, water play, play dough containing different smells ◆ Opportunities for movement to enhance gross and fine motor skills, for example Tumble Tots gym classes, outdoor activities, dough play ◆ Stimulating toys and objects that encourage the child to handle them ◆ Visits to farms, zoos, etc. to widen the child's experiences ◆ Playing games such as 'peek-a-boo' to encourage object permanence ◆ Responding to the child's early attempts at speech

| Pre-operational 2–7 years | The age range of this stage is wide. A child of 2 years will behave very differently to the 7-year-old, but **Piaget** identified this as the stage at which children are not yet able to think in an operational way. He defined operational thought as the ability to think in an orderly, logical manner. Thought processes are developing, but are not yet at the adult stage. **Piaget** considered that for full operational thought to take place children needed the ability to combine schemas. Schemas are the ideas or mental pictures established by a child through interaction with the environment. Schemas will exist for all aspects of life such as 'crossing the road' or 'picking up a book'. Operational thought allows the child to combine schemas in a sensible way that gives children the means to think imaginatively and to consider 'what may happen' if something else occurs. For more about schemas, see pages 47 and 52. Egocentric behaviour is continued from the previous stage where the child is unable to see another person's viewpoint. Children are still unable to conceptualise abstractly but they do at this stage have an increasing ability to symbolise (for example, writing, reading and imaginary play). As this stage progresses, children demonstrate a strong respect for rules. | When considering activities to support Piaget's stages it is important to remember that the pre-operational stage covers a wide age range from 2 to 7 years and that activities need to be appropriate to the child's level of development at the time.
◆ Provision of stimulating activities and experiences to encourage the child to adapt and change his existing view of the world
◆ Provision of activities for number, mass and volume to encourage conservation, for example water play with different size and same size containers, play dough, counting games and number games, cooking and shopping
◆ Giving opportunities for symbolic and 'pretend' play to increase child's ability to use symbols
◆ Making writing materials available
◆ Supporting children to 'see things from other people's point of view'
◆ Supporting children in understanding the idea of sharing
◆ Promoting an 'active' environment for learning that stimulates children to be involved and learn through their experiences first-hand
◆ Playing games that include rules
◆ Arranging paired or small group work to encourage children to listen to another person's point of view/share ideas |

Concrete operations 7–11/12 years	The child is more rational and 'adult-like' in his thought processes. He is able to think logically, although may still need concrete objects to assist with logical thought. Egocentricity is declining. The child is less influenced by the appearance of objects and is able to conserve (i.e. mass, number, length, and area).	◆ Increased opportunity to use logical thought, with concrete materials, for example when learning mathematical concepts ◆ Activities involving problem-solving ◆ More complex literacy and numeric activities
Formal operations 11/12–16 years	Cognitive structures are now more like those of adults. The child is able to use his own ideas to consider problems, to think abstractly and hypothetically. Children are also able to consider different arguments and points of view and to form their own opinions on moral and philosophical issues.	

TRY IT OUT

Using your knowledge of **Piaget**'s *theory, consider the children that you work with. Do the activities and experiences that you provide reflect Piaget's work?*

The legacy of **Piaget**'s work has been to encourage practitioners to provide a stimulating environment that encourages children to learn and to continually develop their understanding and view of the world around them. You must recognise the importance of providing experiences or interactions with the world and encourage children to take an active role in their learning. Children need to develop their own understanding of concepts and build mental structures for themselves. It is not enough to memorise answers and regurgitate someone else's meaning as this will not allow them to transfer their knowledge from one learning situation to another.

As **Piaget** concluded that children's learning is developmentally based, many settings carefully assess each child's stage of cognitive development and plan the curriculum accordingly. This may be done by using observations of the children to build understanding of their knowledge. Activities are then planned that allow children to advance through each developmental stage and encourage them to think about and change previously held concepts.

Schemas

Piaget used specific terms to describe the process that a child goes through in order to develop and change his concepts of the world around him. He believed that a child forms a plan, or schema, in their brain about something he experiences. The schema is a mental structure that enables the child to classify their experiences, initially without words and then with labels as the ability to use language progresses. As the child has wider experiences, the schema is adapted to take into account their changing view of the environment.

Adaptation

The building of schemas involves a process of assimilation where the child takes in information and fits it to the existing schema they have. At some point the information being processed will not fit the existing schema and the child has to adjust their concepts to accommodate the new information. This is known as accommodation and is a response to a feeling of not understanding, or disequilibrium (unbalance). Once the schema has changed, and developed, a state of equilibration takes place. The combined process of assimilation and accommodation is known as adaptation. See the example in the case study below.

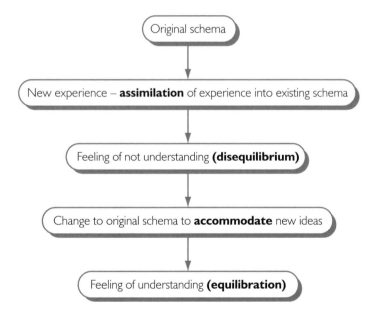

The process of adaptation

CASE STUDY:

MAX AND THE SAND

Max, aged 3, is at the sand tray with one other boy. He is pushing the sand around. The other boy gets in the way and Max pushes him away. No language is used and the other boy leaves the sand tray while Max continues to play.

Max is playing at the sand tray with a blue car. He is burying the car in the sand using his fingers to dig out the sand and cover the entire car. After a while he finds a Brio train which is bigger than the car. He starts to bury the train as well, but finds that he has to use his whole hand to scoop up enough sand to bury it.

A girl comes to the other side of the sand tray and plays alongside Max. They do not speak. Max is concentrating very intently on covering and uncovering his train. The other child leaves. Max does not look up and is not distracted from his play.

Max starts to scoop the sand with a rake, using it like a spade, and buries his train.

In the case study above, Max has an existing schema, burying or enveloping the car in sand. When a larger toy is used, Max has to adapt his original schema. He becomes aware that he will not be able to bury the train in the same way and that he must use a tool. This process shows how Max assimilates the task and adapts his existing schema to accommodate the new information.

TRY IT OUT

Observe a child engaged in an activity that involves them changing their concept of the environment, for example putting shapes into a new shape sorter. Observe the way they approach the problem. Note whether the child adapts the way he or she uses the shape sorter.

In order for children to develop and learn, you need to plan activities that create a state of disequilibrium, although there must be balance between guiding the child and allowing them to explore for themselves and learn by discovery. **Piaget** believed that the adult should act as a guide for children.

Criticisms of Piaget's work

There have been criticisms of **Piaget**'s work:

◆ He used a limited number of children for his research and that his views were therefore too general.

◆ The language Piaget used and the nature of the tests for conservation and egocentricity were too remote for the children. Subsequent research has given different results by using simplified language and more real situations.

◆ Children are able to show understanding of key concepts, such as conservation, at a younger age and stage of development than **Piaget** thought.

In the 1970s **Martin Hughes** recreated the test carried out by **Piaget** to see whether children were egocentric by building a model with dolls – a person and a policeman, rather than a series of mountains. He made the experiment more relevant and appealing to the children by turning it into a game of hide and seek. Most of the 3 and 4-year-old children tested by Hughes were able to imagine themselves in the role of the policeman and of the person.

McGarrigle and **Donaldson** also changed the conservation test by using a 'naughty teddy' glove puppet who changed the position of the row of counters in the number test. When the children were able to join in the test and see it as a game, they mostly realised that the number of counters stayed the same even though the appearance had changed.

Despite these criticisms, **Piaget** remains a major contributor to the way we view children. There is an emphasis on the importance of the environment and the quality of the children's interactions. There is also an acknowledgement that children develop through different stages and therefore the curriculum we provide must reflect these individual differences.

Piaget's influence on modern practice

- Activities should be age- and stage-appropriate.
- Activities should support thinking.
- We should provide children with concrete materials to support thinking. These could include bricks to help when building train tracks or number bars to help children calculate simple addition sums.
- We should provide first-hand, practical experiences. These help children to continue to build mental processes and structures.
- We need to understand children as individuals.
- We should observe children and respond appropriately to them.
- The curriculum needs to be carefully structured to reflect the stage of development the child has reached.
- We should respect a child's need to be active in their learning and to 'learn by doing'.

How you can use Piaget's theory in your work with children

It is important to develop your own practice in line with what you know about how children learn. It is necessary, therefore, to reflect upon the activities and experiences that you provide for children and consider how you can improve provision in order to encourage and extend individual children's learning.

THINK ABOUT IT

Look at the key areas where **Piaget** has influenced modern practice and consider what you provide and how you could extend that provision. You could complete a table like the one below. Some examples have been included.

You will have started to think about the activities you provide and to reflect on the influence of **Piaget** on the choices you make in your setting. For this activity consider carefully the activities you provide and match them to **Piaget**'s ideas. Some examples have been provided but it is important that you reflect upon your own practice and the reason why you are doing things.

Making links between your practice and Piaget's theory

Piaget's influence on modern practice	Activities you provide that promote that aspect of his theory	Further activities and experiences to extend your provision
Plan activities that are age- and stage-appropriate	*Example: matching level of difficulty of jigsaw to child's ability*	*Example: providing harder jigsaws to stretch the child's ability*
Plan activities that support thinking	*Example: what will happen next in the story?*	
Provide children with concrete materials to support thinking	*Example: the song 'Five Currant Buns in a Baker's Shop' – with toy currant buns to take away*	
Provide first-hand, practical experiences	*Example: learning to use scissors*	*Example: increasing the difficulty of the task by cutting different materials*
Understand children as individuals		
Observe children and respond appropriately to them		

Structure the curriculum carefully to reflect the stage of development the child has reached	*Example: reading stories that are appropriate for stage of development*	
Respect a child's need to be active in its learning and to 'learn by doing'	*Example: outdoor play*	*Example: exploring on a trip to the woods*

The activity above will have made you think deeply about the work you are already doing and how to develop and improve that work. You may have reflected upon the way that you lay activities out for the children and thought about the possibility of making activities more open-ended so that children are involved in problem-solving, independent thinking and abstract thought.

You may have asked yourself the following questions:

◆ How do I know the activities I provide are age-appropriate?

◆ What makes me think the children are enjoying active learning?

◆ What do I know about the children as individuals?

◆ Am I giving the children the opportunity for first-hand experiences?

◆ How can I support children with their thinking?

◆ Am I providing the right materials to support thinking?

◆ How do I carry out observations?

◆ Do I use these observations of children to respond appropriately to their needs?

◆ How is the curriculum structured and does it meet the child's developmental needs?

When involved in reflection on your practice, it is always useful to discuss ideas and issues with a colleague or friend. This often helps to cement your understanding and to improve practice. Early years practitioners often discuss their work formally at meetings and also informally during the course of the working day. This form of communication and reflection is important if childcare and education for children is to continue to improve and not remain static.

Piaget's theories are also discussed in the following chapters:

◆ *Chapter 3, Children's communication, page 73*

◆ *Chapter 4, Children's relationships, page 107.*

Recent research on schemas

Modern researchers, including **Tina Bruce**, have continued to look at the way children learn and consider the implications for practice. They have built upon the work of **Piaget**, particularly with regard to schemas. Their work has deepened understanding so that we now recognise the schemas, or patterns, that a child demonstrates through their actions, language or play that enable them to learn and to assimilate and accommodate new information.

> 'Schemas are patterns of linked behaviours which the child can generalise and use in a whole variety of different situations. It is best to think of schemas as a cluster of pieces which fit together.'
>
> *Source: Bruce (1996)*

There is still a lot for practitioners to learn about schemas, but by watching children play with a variety of toys and materials, an observant practitioner will notice that there is a pattern emerging that links apparently dissimilar activities. Children show interest in certain activities which they repeat again and again in different situations. Common schemas include:

◆ trajectory and rotation

◆ enveloping

◆ connecting

◆ transporting.

Common schemas

Schema	Description
Trajectory Moving in or representing straight lines, arcs or curves. 	Children who are interested in trajectories enjoy being very active by running, climbing, jumping, throwing and catching balls. They are fascinated by movement and direction, so will enjoy playing with pulleys and ball games. They will be interested in rockets, planets and space, train tracks and moving trains.

Rotation Children are interested in rotational movement.	Rotation schemas are demonstrated by a fascination with things that go round. Children will often like to play with wheeled toys, hoops, balls, spinning and riding round and round the playground on a tricycle or sit-on toy. They may be interested in unlocking and locking doors with keys, turning taps on and off. Drawings may show spirals and circles.
Connecting Children make connections between items and enjoy construction	Children enjoy using construction materials and making models using sellotape, stapling, tubes and boxes. They will be interested in woodwork, water play, kites and pull along toys.
Transporting Children moving articles from one place to another, for example dolls in prams, sticks in a truck to make a bonfire, collecting shells on the beach to put on the sandcastle	Children fill bags, prams, wheelbarrows and then transport them to other places. They may describe their play as 'going on holiday' or 'having a picnic'. Furniture may be rearranged. Transporting is often associated with enveloping.
Enveloping Children are seen to enjoy covering themselves and exploring under and inside	Children enjoy covering themselves, crawling inside tunnels and under blankets. They like to go inside tents, sheds and playhouses. They may paint pictures and then cover them over with black paint saying it is night time. Children often like to write letters, folding and putting them inside an envelope.

Source: www.wallhall.herts.sch.uk

There are other identified schemas and you may wish to research these for yourself to increase your understanding of how children learn.

How do practitioners use their knowledge of schemas?

A good example using schemas is the Pen Green Centre in the case study below. Other sources of information are identified in the References section at the end of this chapter.

> ### CASE STUDY:
> ### THE PEN GREEN CENTRE FOR UNDER FIVES AND THEIR FAMILIES
>
> The Pen Green Centre is committed to working with parents to understand the role of schemas in children's learning.
>
> The practitioners work closely together, and with the parents or carers, to understand individual children's schemas. Regular meetings are held to discuss the children and their current activity and to share how to support the child in their learning.
>
> The practitioners are very aware that by supporting the child and valuing their interests they will be enhancing and promoting self-esteem and self-discipline. They recognise that a child will thrive in a setting where the adults work well together and value the child's contribution.
>
> Regular observations are carried out, shared between practitioners and parents, and the curriculum is then planned to provide the children with appropriate and flexible activities that will allow them to grow. The curriculum is arranged to cover all aspects of learning, recognising that children learn in an integrated, rather than isolated, way. Materials are provided, exploration is structured and the child is encouraged to make choices and decisions, acknowledging the importance of autonomy for the child.
>
> It is recognised at Pen Green that children are born to learn and that adults only need to know how best to help them. The role of the adult is to observe the child carefully, recognise what the child is serious about and discover their schema. Observations provide the adult with the information they need in order to provide activities to consolidate and extend learning in whatever direction the child takes. It helps the adult enhance what the child does naturally in worthwhile directions.
>
> Details of the work of the centre are available on their website (www.pengreen.org).

How you can use the knowledge of children's schemas in your work with children

In order to understand children's schemas, you will need to perfect the skill of observing children in a way that enhances your knowledge of the child. This involves a lot of practice on your part to master different methods of observation and to perfect the techniques of recording children's movements and language without disrupting or disturbing their play. The ability to observe children will enable you to build your knowledge of individual children and to reflect on ways to extend their learning.

> ### TRY IT OUT
>
> *Have you ever watched children and realised that they keep playing in a similar way? Why do they do that?*
>
> *Observe a group of children playing independently over a period of time.*
>
> ◆ *Are they showing an interest in particular activities?*
> ◆ *Can you see a pattern emerging?*
> ◆ *Does their behaviour link to a recognised schema?*
>
> *You may wish to confirm your observations with colleagues or parents/carers and discuss the schemas you see emerging.*

Providing support for children's schemas can be very rewarding for the child and for you. The child's self-esteem will be enhanced by knowing that adults recognise the importance of their activities and value them. The child will benefit emotionally from the interest taken in them and may respond by demonstrating a fascination for specific activities that continues into later life. It would be interesting to ask adults about their interests as children and see whether those interests are reflected in current career choices or hobbies.

If you become aware of a schema that interests the child, it is useful to use this information when planning activities to stimulate development. Children, like adults, are more likely to respond positively to an activity that fascinates them. Adults can support the schema by providing appropriate materials, activities and challenges that sensitively encourage learning. They can also support schemas by using appropriate language that introduces new vocabulary and encourages the child to comment on the world. When adults understand the schema and focus of the child's interest, the discussions they have will be more genuine and plausible to the child. Children know when adults are only half interested or don't really know what they are talking about.

> ### TRY IT OUT
>
> *Using your observations of children, choose one child to work with.*
>
> ◆ *Consider what you know about their interests and the schemas that are evident in their play. How will this knowledge inform your planning?*
> ◆ *What activities and experiences would you provide to develop knowledge and understanding for the child?*
> ◆ *Consider the language you may introduce.*
>
> *You may find it useful to compare your answers with the suggestions in the table below.*

Suggested activities and experiences to develop schemas

Schema	Activities and experiences to encourage development of the schema What can I provide that will help children to learn? What words can I introduce them to?
Trajectory	Use of cars and vehicles moving along roadways. Remote control cars that move in different directions. (Initially the child will only be able to deal with one direction.) Opportunities to work with pulleys and to move sand and water up and down. Trains and train tracks to show movement backwards and forwards and movement along a line. Trip to a station or viaduct. *Vocabulary*: up and down, backwards, forwards, straight, north, south, east, west, viaduct, signals, sidings.
Rotation	Provide the child with experiences that involve rotation – trips to the London Eye or on roundabouts at the fair. Give opportunity to use a simple potter's wheel or colour wheel. Provide spinners and tops in the classroom and hoops, roundabouts or helter skelters outside. Allow the child to experiment with locks and keys and taps safely. *Vocabulary*: rotates, roundabout, circles, circular, spinning, spirals.
Connecting	Provide the child with opportunities to make connections – Knex, Lego and making models with cardboard, glue, sellotape and scissors. Give them string and rope to tie things together and let them help hanging out the washing. Provide opportunities to make and fly kites and use pull along toys. Encourage technology skills and use of tools to construct models. *Vocabulary*: joining, connecting, connections, pulling, pushing, links.
Transporting	Materials to transport, for example sand and water, stones. Simple and complex systems for moving water and sand. Provision of buckets and containers, pipes and funnels and containers to transport materials such as wheelbarrows and trolleys, trainers on bikes. Building using a marble run. Visits to a water wheel or swimming pool with flumes. Observing a boat going through a lock, car transporters being loaded up. *Vocabulary*: moving, transporting, sliding, filling up, pouring
Enveloping	Opportunities to cover objects such as wrapping presents for Christmas and birthdays. Encourage concepts of space and size – how much paper do we need to cover the present? Provide assortment of boxes with lids, and interesting dressing-up clothes. Give children the opportunity to make wigwams and tents and build homes from old sheets and large pieces of material. Play Kim's game where objects are put on a tray and covered up. The child is then asked to recall the items on the tray. *Vocabulary*: covering, enveloping, wrapper, layer, casing.

Observing children's schemas is an important tool for you to use to further your understanding of how the child learns through their fascinations and interests. To achieve the maximum potential of this knowledge, you must think carefully how to support the child and enhance learning. **Bruce** is clear about how beneficial she believes the contribution of schemas to be to a child's learning and development through:

◆ the socio-cultural context in which they develop

◆ the support to children in what they know

◆ the extension of children's understanding

◆ the enhancement of children's uniqueness

◆ the ability to modify, change and transform as they develop

◆ the common ground that is identified trans-globally in children's play and learning

◆ helping adults to tune in to the child's world

◆ helping practitioners to develop best practice in an evolutionary way

◆ helping practitioners to link and find shared ground without becoming standardised and uniform in practice

◆ helping us to celebrate with parents the human and cultural diversity of children and their lives.

Source: Adapted from Bruce (1997), page 103

It is also possible to see how early examples of a child's schemas develop into later concepts and **Bruce** highlights these (see the table below).

Development of concepts from early schemas

Early schema	Later concept
Vertical trajectory	Height
Horizontal trajectory	Length, timelines in history
Lateral trajectory	Angles
Enclosure	Maps. Geometry, regular shapes, art, figure drawing
Envelopment	Surrounding and covering, area in mathematics, greenhouses in biology and horticulture, hot air balloons and the physics of gases, concept of run-off in geography as in rain running down a slope, camouflage colour and shading in art
Containers	Capacity and volume
Transporting	Quantity and understanding of number

Source: Adapted from Bruce (1997), page 79

Bruce's theories are also discussed in the following chapters:

◆ *early social interaction, Chapter 3, page 85*

◆ *supporting early literacy, Chapter 3, page 92*

◆ *free-flow play, Chapter 6, page 177.*

Lev Vygotsky

Lev Vygotsky (1896–1934)

The role of the adult in the development of children's learning was recognised by the work of **Piaget** and has been further developed by other researchers. **Lev Vygotsky**, working in Russia in the early twentieth century, developed the idea that the adult is there to guide the child's learning and to assist the child to move forward in their understanding. **Vygotsky** saw the importance of social interactions and maintained that the child was able to develop intellectually through significant input from adults and peers working alongside the child.

This research has had a huge influence on the way we work with children today. Early years practitioners are aware of the need to provide opportunities for social interaction and to consider carefully the quality of the input from adults and significant others.

Vygotsky's work has encouraged the modern practitioner to focus on providing challenge for the child through activities and experiences that stretch the child to think above their capabilities. The child is able to work within their own capabilities in the zone of actual development, but with assistance from adults or more skilled peers they are able to extend their thoughts and work within the zone of proximal development. This zone of proximal development can be defined as the difference between what a child can do alone and what a child can do with help.

> ## TRY IT OUT
>
> *At this point, you may find it useful to draw a diagram to show your understanding of the zone of actual development and the zone of proximal development.*

Many schools and early years settings encourage children to work and play together in an informal way, but some settings have also established more formalised schemes such as paired reading and mentoring that reflect **Vygotsky**'s theories of learning.

CASE STUDY:
KEVIN AND THE TOWER

Kevin has been interested in building towers from bricks for some weeks. He has been using bricks and designing the tallest tower he can. Sammy and Johan have joined him and the three children have spent the morning finding all the bricks in the nursery. However, they are getting frustrated that the tower falls over when it gets to 12 bricks high.

An early years practitioner has been observing the children and decides that they need a 'helping hand'. She finds pictures of tall structures and talks to them about how the structures have a firm and sturdy base; they also look at bridges and discuss how different shaped bricks are sturdier than others. This leads to the children experimenting with the design of structures using different combinations of shaped bricks.

Time is also spent discussing and observing buildings around the nursery site and the children soon notice that tall buildings need to be 'stuck' together to give them the necessary strength. The practitioner arranges for the children to visit a building site and watch workers building a wall.

By carefully observing the children and noticing their level of understanding, the practitioner has been able to assist the children to work in the zone of proximal development.

It is interesting to observe children involved in pretend or imaginative play as they will assume roles that are beyond their level of actual development, playing characters such as a parent, car driver or shop assistant. Through play they are putting themselves in the zone of proximal development and playing at a level that is beyond their true capabilities.

Like **Piaget**, **Vygotsky** believed that children need opportunities to build mental structures that help them to understand and process the world around them. These mental structures are assisted in their development by the use of language. Therefore, it is important for children to have the opportunity to extend their understanding and use of language as a communication tool and to help them master higher mental functions.

A recent research project funded by the DfES (1997–2003) called the Effective Pre-School and Primary Education 3–11 Project (EPPE) focused on the effectiveness of early years education. They found that quality interactions between children and adults, and children and children, are particularly important when solving intellectual problems and on a 1:1 basis.

The zone of proximal development is also discussed in Chapter 4, page 111.

How do practitioners use Vygotsky's theory of learning?

Evidence of **Vygotsky**'s theory is seen in schools and nurseries today where adults are aware of the importance of their role in assisting children to move beyond their own capabilities, the zone of actual development, and to work at a higher level in the zone of proximal development. Practitioners recognise **Vygotsky**'s view that the role of the adult in education is crucial in order to help the child develop the necessary abilities to be a successful learner. The most effective way to encourage a child's natural abilities is to encourage them to work in the zone of proximal development by providing challenge in the activities they do.

CASE STUDY:

SHINING EYES AND BUSY MINDS

Galina Dolya and David Higgins established a pre-school group for children, in Hertfordshire, based on putting the theories of Vygotsky into practice alongside the latest worldwide research into children's learning. The setting, Shining Eyes and Busy Minds, aims to encourage learning in children of a young age, fostering an enthusiasm that stays with them for life.

David Higgins had been troubled by the lack of 'buzz' for children in education in England and had travelled to Russia to the Eureka University to see for himself how children were being motivated and to observe their enthusiasm for knowledge. The work that David saw there was impressive and led him to establish a setting in England, with Galina, for pre-school children.

Their work acknowledges that the period of brain development from birth to 5 years is crucial in developing children who are able, confident and enthusiastic learners. Based on the work of Leonid Venger (a student of Vygotsky), Galina has developed a course, Key to Learning, which identifies the mental tools children need to think and communicate and identifies a systematic process to develop them. This course works on the idea that all children can be supported to succeed in formal education by carefully structured and supported work in the early years of their development. The aim is to create the conditions for 'minds to open, for learning to become a pleasure, and for creativity to flourish'.

The environment at Shining Eyes and Busy Minds is alive with child-initiated activities and is rich in materials and experiences that encourage the children to problem-solve and learn from their experiences. There are also carefully structured small group sessions that enable the adults to introduce activities to the children that develop a wide range of skills and learning styles. The children show a keen and motivated attitude to learning. Over 150 schools and nurseries in the UK now use the Key to Learning programmes.

There are 12 modules involved in Key to Learning ranging from Story Grammar to Sensory Maths. More detailed information is available on the website (www. keytolearning.com) or by email (keytolearning@fsmail.net). There is also a teacher's TV programme *Laying the Foundations of Literacy*.

Examples of the programme are available on the website and give some idea of the nature of the work they do and the experiences they provide. An example of a week's activity for the Butterfly group is shown opposite.

BUTTERFLIES

MONDAY	**CONSTRUCTION**	**Construction of Decorative Gateways** 1. To teach children to single out the main elements of a construction through analysing a plan (linear diagram). 2. To enable children to plan actions and decide in advance the sequence of building and the order in which bricks will be used.
TUESDAY	**STORY GRAMMAR**	**Little Red Riding Hood** 1. To extend the use of substitutes in retelling the story. 2. To organise substitutes in the correct sequence to represent the key points in a story.
TUESDAY	**MODELLING**	**Children in the Wood** 1. To teach children to complete and transform a familiar art composition. 2. To enable children to recognise and remove unwanted objects and construct the image of a new object.
WEDNESDAY	**EXPLORATION**	**The Kingdom of Ice, Water and Steam** 1. To reinforce the knowledge of the transformation of the states of water. 2. To develop an understanding of the signs and symbols for ice, water and steam.
WEDNESDAY	**LOGIC**	**Clever questions** 1. To teach children to name correctly all four attributes of a hidden shape. 2. To use logic signs and symbols as a plan for asking questions.
WEDNESDAY	**DEVELOPMENTAL GAMES**	**Who will become What?** 1. To understand the concept of change and growth. 2. To realise that there are sometimes several possible answers to the same question.
THURSDAY	**VISUAL – SPATIAL**	**Train Journey** 1. To teach children to move in a direction as indicated by an arrow. 2. To use symbols (arrows) to indicate a route on a map.
THURSDAY	**EXPRESSIVE MOVEMENT**	**Sad – Happy** 1. To introduce methods of showing the character's mood by the corresponding gestures. 2. To develop imagination by mastering actions with imaginary objects.
FRIDAY	**MATHEMATICS**	**Game with Balloons** 1. To observe and understand the action of reversal and the action of serialisation using balloons. 2. To demonstrate the transitional state of a balloon during the process of inflation from small to large.
FRIDAY	**ARTOGRAPHICS**	**Soap Bubbles** 1. To teach and draw circles of various sizes on paper, filling the spaces with dots without touching or entering the circles. 2. To develop graphic abilities in writing by guided and free drawing, copying teacher's movements and not only the pattern.

An example of a week's activity in the Key to Learning programme

The influence of Vygotsky's work on current practice

Vygotsky's work has impacted on learning in numerous ways:

◆ It shows the importance of children learning through interaction with adults and peers.

◆ It emphasises the importance of the adult role in helping children to perform tasks they are incapable of performing alone.

◆ The assessment of children's abilities must take into account the zone of proximal development, acknowledging the difference between what a child can do alone and what they can do with help.

◆ It recognises the importance of language in enabling the child to make sense of their world and also in assisting the adult to transmit knowledge to the child.

How you can use Vygotsky's theory in your work with children

You will already have started to consider your own role when working with children in terms of the activities and experiences you provide and the strategies you use to meet the child's needs and to enhance learning. It is also important to reflect upon the way you work and how you interact with children in order to assist them to work within the zone of proximal development.

THINK ABOUT IT

◆ What do you do that helps children?

◆ What can they do with your help that they cannot do alone?

◆ Do you interact with children in a way that extends their ability to learn?

◆ Do you provide challenges for children?

◆ When have you helped children to work in their zone of proximal development?

You may wish to discuss these points with a colleague.

Vygotsky's theories are also discussed in the following chapters:

◆ *the relationship between language and thought, Chapter 3, page 78*

◆ *children's relationships, Chapter 4, page 113*

◆ *children's play, Chapter 6, page 173.*

Jerome Bruner

Jerome Bruner is one of the most influential and best-known psychologists of current times and has been a key figure in education since the 1960s. His theory of cognitive growth has shown the importance of the environment and social and cultural factors in a child's learning. He views children as active problem solvers,

Jerome Bruner (1915–)

eager and ready to explore difficult subjects with the help of stimulating and intuitive teachers. In **Bruner**'s view, humans have the ability to learn and grow with no limit to their potential. Anything can be taught to anyone at any age, the important factor is how it is taught.

There is a strong link between the work of **Vygotsky** and **Bruner** in that both theorists stress the importance of the partnership between the adult and the child for successful learning. **Bruner** considers that it is necessary for the adult to be able to ascertain what the child can do without help, but also it is important to know what the child can achieve with help.

CASE STUDY:

LEZA LEARNING TO WALK

Leza had always preferred to sit and play with her toys. She was not particularly interested in learning to walk and at 13 months had not yet crawled or pulled herself up on her feet. She was content to sit for long periods of time, quietly investigating the contents of a large tin filled with small interesting items and playing with other toys on the carpet. Her parents felt some concerns that there may be a physical reason why Leza was not walking.

However, this did not mean Leza was unable to walk; simply that she needed some assistance and incentive to do so. Her parents resolved to teach her to walk before her next assessment at the health clinic. With sensitive encouragement from her family, she quickly learned to pull herself up and eventually to walk around the house and garden holding the hand of anyone who was available. The family did this by giving her toys that she could push along, such as a new buggy for her favourite doll, by encouraging her to hold their hands and showing her interesting things to motivate her and stimulate the need to walk.

The term 'scaffolding' is used by **Bruner** to refer to the adult's ability to assist the child to develop in ways that would be impossible unaided. This, appropriately, conjures up the idea of the adult building scaffolding around the child in order to help them learn a skill. When the child achieves success, the adult gradually removes the scaffolding until the child is competent alone.

Bruner sees learning as a continual process, occurring through three stages:

1   *Enactive* – children need to handle concrete objects in order to understand, for example counting objects by touching them.

2   *Iconic* – learners can represent concepts graphically or mentally, for example they can carry out addition sums in their head.

3   *Symbolic* – learners are able to use logic, higher order thinking skills and symbol systems, for example scientific formulae.

The skills and knowledge required for learning to take place are built up gradually through interaction with the environment and through 'discovery learning', where the child has the opportunity to discover knowledge on their own and to learn through trial and error and their own mistakes. The child must also be given the opportunity to interact with teachers/adults in order to be able to discuss what they have found out and to cement and further their knowledge.

Another aspect of **Bruner**'s theory is the concept of the spiral curriculum. This recognises that in order for learning to take place, children may need to revisit subjects and aspects of learning. This does not mean doing topics on the Romans every year in primary school, but it does mean that adults need to plan for opportunities that enable children to reinforce and cement their understanding of key issues.

THINK ABOUT IT

Reflect upon a new topic that you have recently studied – it could be a language, sport or a hobby.

◆ What did you learn about first?

◆ Did you understand everything immediately?

◆ Did you have to revisit some of the first things you were taught?

◆ Were some aspects easier to understand than others?

◆ Did you find it easier to understand the second, third or fourth time you met the topic?

The difficulty you face is recognising when a child needs to revisit the curriculum and when they are bored with a subject and need to move on. It is important to ensure that children continue to learn from their experiences.

How do practitioners use Bruner's theory of learning?

> ### CASE STUDY:
> ### JOSEPH'S MUSEUM
>
> Joseph, aged 7, was fascinated by pebbles, stones, crystals and fossils and had collected a large assortment of examples, which he kept in a box. However, he was not content with this – he wanted people to be able to see his collection and admire it. With the help of an adult, he decided to create a museum.
>
>
>
> Over several weeks, Joseph and the adult built display cabinets out of boxes and toilet rolls and wrote signs, notices and labels. Eventually a museum was created, complete with opening times and conducted educational tours. Joseph was thrilled, particularly when his first visitors arrived to view his collection.
>
> *Joseph and his museum*

From the case study above, we can see the importance of the adult role in scaffolding learning. Joseph was able to make progress with his museum only with adult help. The experience of working together enabled Joseph to have a fun learning experience and to take this activity to a deeper level.

Adults in a school, nursery or pre-school setting are providing this type of scaffolding for children's learning all the time. Sometimes this involves being aware of the child's interests and responding appropriately with materials, expertise and activities. At other times, it involves discussion and questions. It can also mean that the adult carefully structures the curriculum to provide opportunity for the child to discover knowledge for themselves.

How you can use Bruner's theory in your work with children

The following case study will give you an insight into scaffolding children's learning.

CASE STUDY:

TASNIM PLAYING WITH THE BUG

Tasnim, aged 4, was busy in the nursery computer room. Her friend Adam had found some remote-controlled bugs on the floor and the two of them were busy trying to get them to work. Tasnim pressed the green button on the top of the bug, but the bug did not move. Adam's started to move at once.

'How did you do that?' asks Tasnim.

'I just pressed the button,' replies Adam, and he points to the button.

Tasnim tries hers again but still nothing happens. 'Why won't mine work? You have mine and I'll have yours,' she says, and they swap.

Adam tries the bug but it still won't work. 'I bet it has run out of batteries,' he says.

Tasnim says, 'Try a new one. Look, mine's moving on its own. Look, look,' and she presses the button several times. (It has been pre-programmed so it only moves a small amount.)

Tasnim then finds another bug for Adam but it won't go either. She turns it over and looks at the on/off button. 'It's on, but it won't go because it doesn't have a battery' she tells him. Then she continues playing with her own bug. The adult in the room tells her that she can clear the memory and make the bug go anywhere she wants it to.

Mischa walks into the room and Tasnim tells her that only one of the bugs is working, as it is the only one with a battery. She lifts up one of the other bugs, 'Look at this. It hasn't got a battery in it so it won't work.' She presses the button to demonstrate to Mischa, then she presses hers again and it goes. The adult asks her if she remembered to clear the memory again. 'Oh no,' she replies and laughs, then clears the memory and starts again.

The practitioner plays a key role in the child's learning in this case study. An experience has been provided that encourages the children to work together and discuss what is happening. The adult is on hand to scaffold the learning by providing information and advice at the appropriate moment and to assist the child to move forward with her knowledge and understanding of how bugs work. Tasnim's friend, Adam, has also been instrumental in helping Tasnim to understand why the bug will not work, showing the importance of peer support too.

THINK ABOUT IT

- ◆ What activities would you provide to ensure further learning takes place?
- ◆ How could you extend Tasnim's knowledge of batteries or remote-controlled toys?
- ◆ What is the role of language in this case study?
- ◆ How does this fit in with **Bruner**'s idea of the spiral curriculum?
- ◆ How does this case study link to the work of **Vygotsky** and the zone of proximal development or to **Piaget**'s views on adaptation?

You may have considered providing different activities with toys that are battery-powered or setting up an interactive display of battery-powered objects. With care, you could show children how to put batteries into the object. Further activities with remote-controlled toys could also be provided and discussions initiated with the children about items in the home that are controlled remotely or that need batteries.

You will also have noted that by providing similar activities and experiences, you are encouraging the child to revisit their understanding of batteries and to consolidate and build upon their knowledge. This reflects **Bruner**'s idea of the spiral curriculum.

When reading the case study above, it is easy to see the role of Adam in assisting Tasnim to work outside her own knowledge and to move into the zone of proximal development. The practitioner does not interrupt or join in the conversation between them, which acknowledges the importance of the peer's role in learning. During this case study, Tasnim is changing her view of the bug and how it works, she is assimilating and accommodating the new information she has so that she can adapt her understanding, in line with the work of **Piaget**.

Bruner's theories are also discussed in the following chapters:

◆ *children's communication, Chapter 3, page 79*

◆ *supporting early literacy, Chapter 3, page 93*

◆ *children's relationships, Chapter 4, page 113.*

The role of the early years practitioner in promoting learning

At the beginning of this chapter, it was noted that you need to have knowledge about the way that children learn in order to provide appropriate activities and experiences to extend and develop learning. Understanding of the work of researchers, such as **Piaget**, **Vygotsky** and **Bruner**, enables you to see why you are doing things and gives insight into how to assist the child effectively.

You will find that your knowledge of how children learn does not stand still. You will continue to develop understanding about children as a result of your own experiences and of other people's research. You may also wish to conduct your own small-scale research. Early years practitioners who aim to provide quality education for the children in their care will take part in continuous professional development and in reflective discussions with colleagues. It is important to develop a culture of reflective practice within each setting that continually questions the child's experience of the provision.

CASE STUDY:

REFLECTIVE PRACTICE AT WOO PRE-SCHOOL

Susie Woo runs a playgroup for children aged 2½ years to 4 years old. The group has 25 children at present and there are three full-time members of staff and two part-time. All staff members are qualified to level 3 and have a range of experience from newly qualified to a member of staff who has been working at the pre-school since 1975.

Susie is keen for the staff to share good practice and to develop an atmosphere of reflective discussion. She is aware that it is easy to slip into a pattern of providing the same equipment each day and to forget how to stimulate the children's learning. Adults may establish a repetitive routine that is simple for them to administer but doesn't necessarily create a positive learning environment for the children.

Staff members are therefore encouraged to do simple observations on the children in the group on a regular basis and to share their findings at the end of each session with their colleagues. These observations show the development of individual children and their interest and involvement in the activities offered. The observations then provide a basis for future planning and all the staff are involved in this.

There are also regular opportunities for the staff to get together and reflect on the effectiveness of the experiences provided. This has led to some stimulating discussion on the merits of different aspects of the provision, how to engage all the children in the activities and the need to constantly assess the learning potential of equipment.

Staff also involve the children in discussion about the activities by talking to them about what they enjoy at the pre-school and what they have learnt. Susie takes lots of photographs, with parents' permission, and these provide an excellent stimulus for discussion with the children.

As a result of the staff observations, it has become apparent that only a few children are using the small world activity toys and that none of the children stay at this activity for more than five minutes. None of the children expressed an interest in the toys. When the staff reflected on this at their meeting, they decided that the toys needed to be updated and that the children could be involved in choosing some new toys from the catalogues. There was also considerable discussion about how the toys could provide challenge for the children in order to stimulate learning.

Consider:

1   How do you share good practice with colleagues?

2   Do you use observations to understand children's learning needs better?

3   How do you reflect on the provision at your setting and the learning potential of activities?

4   What would you suggest to Susie and her team?

The case study above demonstrates how important it is for all members of staff to reflect on their practice and to discuss their provision if they are to stimulate learning. It also highlights the use of observations as a tool for understanding children.

TRY IT OUT

Observe an activity area in your setting throughout the length of the session or over a week if possible.

◆ *Note the number of children who use the activity.*
◆ *Look at the learning that is taking place and decide if the children are stimulated by the experience.*
◆ *How involved are the children? Are they concentrating? Are they working together? Are they enjoying the experience?*
◆ *How could practitioners improve the learning experience for the children?*

By continually thinking about your practice and assessing the impact your work has on the children in your care, you will be able to provide children with the right environment to encourage learning.

Reflective questions

To be a reflective practitioner, you need to ask yourself some questions:

◆ Reflect upon your own role in the setting. What is my role? What kind of practitioner am I? How could I improve my practice?

◆ Think about your future development. How can I improve my knowledge of children? What kind of practitioner do I want to be in the future?

◆ Why do I provide the activities and experiences for the children I work with? What are they learning from them? Are they learning anything?

◆ What can I provide for the children that will enhance their learning? How can I make learning fun and stimulating?

◆ What are the children's individual needs? How can I find out what interests individuals? What do I know about each child's development?

◆ How do colleagues see me as a practitioner? Am I working effectively with my colleagues to provide quality education for the children?

◆ When can I reflect on my practice?

◆ How will I use reflection in my future planning for the children?

Summary

The role of the practitioner in early years care and education is complex and involves reflection, observation skills and knowledge of children. You need to have an in-depth knowledge of child development and the theory behind how children learn. You also need to be able to plan appropriately for progression of learning and to extend young children. It is also imperative to be able to work alongside colleagues through effective communication and interpersonal skills.

In this chapter we have looked at a number of theories of how children learn and have identified how these theories impact on the modern practice seen in numerous settings. The emphasis has been on the work of **Piaget**, **Vygotsky** and **Bruner** and on recent research into the role of schemas in children's learning, including **Bruce**. The chapter has outlined the key components of each theoretical perspective and encouraged you to reflect on how this influences your own practice. We have also considered how you can improve and extend the learning activities and experiences offered to the children.

Each theorist's work represents differences and similarities in approach. **Piaget** sees the child developing principally in stages and that mental ability is tied to those stages. There is very little mention of the social development of the child. **Vygotsky** agreed with much of **Piaget**'s thoughts, but placed an emphasis on social development, noting the importance of adults and peers in promoting development and allowing the child to move into zones of development that were inaccessible alone. **Bruner**'s work also reflects the importance of the adult in forming the child's progress with learning through his views on scaffolding and the spiral curriculum.

If you have found this interesting, there are many other examples of research and theory that you could study for yourself. You may, for example, want to consider the work of **Freud**, **Erikson**, **Pavlov** or **Skinner**. There is also work by **Piaget** and **Kohlberg** on the way children learn the rules of morality, the difference between right and wrong. The list is endless.

Skinner's theories are discussed in Chapter 3 (Children's communication), page 75, and Chapter 6, page 176.

Freud is discussed in Chapter 4 (Children's relationships), pages 109 and 136, and Chapter 5 (How children feel), page 161.

CHECK YOUR UNDERSTANDING

1   What is your understanding of the stages of development outlined by **Piaget**?

2   Consider the ages of the children you are working with. Does their behaviour fit in with **Piaget**'s theories?

3   What are the key features of **Vygotsky**'s work?

4   What does scaffolding mean?

5   Do you understand what a schema is? How does this apply to your work with children?

6   What do you consider to be your role as a practitioner?

7   If you reflect upon your practice, what do you think you could improve?

References and further reading

Athey, C. (1990) *Extending Thought in Young Children*, Paul Chapman Publications

Brain, C. and Mukherji, P. (2005) *Understanding Child Psychology*, Nelson Thornes

Bruce, T. (1997) *Early Childhood Education*, 2nd edition, Hodder & Stoughton

Bruner, J. (1983) 'Education as social invention', *Journal of Social Issues*, Vol. 39, pp129–41

Daly, M., Byers, E. and Taylor, W. (2004) *Early Years Management in Practice*, Heinemann

Davenport, G.C. (1988) *An Introduction to Child Development*, Collins Educational

Flanagan, C. (1996) *Applying Psychology to Early Child Development*, Hodder & Stoughton

Lindon, J. (2005) *Understanding Child Development: Linking Theory and Practice*, Hodder Arnold

Tassoni, P., Beith, K. and Eldridge, H. (2000) *Diploma in Child Care and Education*, Heinemann

Tassoni, P. and Hucker, K. (2005) *Planning Play and the Early Years*, 2nd edition, Heinemann

Useful websites

www.pengreen.org

www.childrens-mathematics.co.uk

http://evolution.massey.ac.nz

http://health.enotes.com/childrens-health-encyclopedia/cognitive-development

www.keytolearning.com

www.standards.dfes.gov.uk

www.surestart.gov.uk

Chapter 3

Children's communication

Introduction

In this chapter we will look at the some of the theoretical perspectives on how children acquire language. We will also look at other ways in which children communicate and how you might support these communications.

Babies begin to communicate from the moment they are born. Young children use a variety of ways to communicate with each other, the adults who care for them and with the wider world. An essential ingredient of becoming a reflective practitioner is to constantly evaluate the way in which you communicate with children and explore ways in which you can make the communication more effective. As a practitioner trained to support children's learning and development, you will also need to ascertain what is best practice in supporting children's communication skills. In order to do this you need to examine not just language as a form of communication but also non-verbal communication, acquisition of language and emerging literacy in young children.

In this chapter we will look at the some of the theoretical perspectives on how children acquire language. Theorists over the years have been exploring the ways in which children learn to speak and the findings from their research have influenced and informed the way in which we encourage and support children in their earliest communications. We will also look at other ways in which children communicate and the ways in which you might support these communications.

This chapter covers:

- ◆ How children learn to speak
- ◆ The importance of early social interaction
- ◆ Supporting children in early literacy.

The theorists and researchers covered in this chapter are:

◆ **B.F. Skinner**, page 75

◆ **Noam Chomsky**, page 76

◆ **Lois Bloom**, page 77

◆ **Margaret Donaldson**, page 78

◆ **Michael Halliday**, pages 79 and 89

◆ **Jerome Bruner**, pages 79 and 93

◆ **Lev Vygotsky**, page 78

◆ **Jean Piaget**, page 78

◆ **H. Rudolf Schaffer**, page 81

◆ **Marian Whitehead**, pages 82 and 96

◆ **Tina Bruce**, pages 85 and 92

◆ **Gopnik et al.**, page 87

◆ **Jeni Riley** and **David Reedy**, page 90 and 100

◆ **Abraham Maslow**, page 92.

How children learn to speak

The ability to use language as a form of communication sets human beings apart from all the animal species. Young children rapidly learn how to speak in the early years and there continues to be a great deal of research into children's acquisition of language. Theorists and linguists have always been fascinated by the way children acquire language in a seemingly effortless way.

We will explore how children acquire language through looking at the key theories and approaches:

◆ the behaviourist approach

◆ the nativist approach

◆ the semantic approach

◆ the interactionist approach.

Very often these approaches are looked at in unison as one merges into the other, but we will look at them separately for now, exploring other theories and ideas later.

The behaviourist approach

B.F. Skinner (1904–90)

B.F. Skinner published a book in 1957 called *Verbal Behaviour*, in which he explained his views on how language is acquired. He based his views on research conducted on animals – you may have heard of **Skinner**'s rat experiments. He looked at the process of response and reward in these experiments with rats and applied some of these to the principles of learning language. He told us that children are 'empty vessels' and are born waiting for us to fill them up with language through the parents' nurturing of the child. He said that it was no different from any other form of learning, a process of stimulus, response and reinforcement, shown in the diagram below.

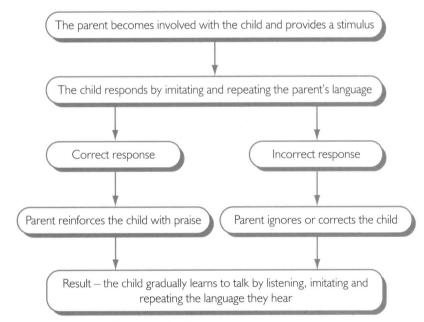

Skinner's process of nurturing language development

This viewpoint would seem to make sense, as we hear young children imitating and copying adults speech all the time. However, this does not explain *why* children say things that an adult would never say. For example, John aged 3 said:

◆ 'I *hurted mineself* when *mine* did fall over.'
◆ 'I fell off the bike my daddy *gived* to me.'

You would probably agree that an adult would not use this sort of language and so **Skinner**'s theory left us with some unanswered questions about how children learn how to speak. However, such a strong behaviourist approach as **Skinner**'s is not common today.

Skinner is also discussed in Chapter 6, page 176.

The nativist approach

Noam Chomsky wrote a criticism of **Skinner**'s work in 1959 and claimed that his theory was flawed. He said that rats could not be used when studying the learning of language and that **Skinner** had misunderstood the nature of language. He claimed **Skinner** had not taken into account two things that were really important about language:

◆ Nearly every sentence that a person says is a different combination of words and therefore children could not only learn language by learning correct responses.

◆ Children develop complex ways of speaking without any formal coaching and think of new ways to construct sentences to make themselves understood.

Chomsky told us that these two fundamental facts demonstrated that human beings are born with an innate predisposition to learn language. He called this the language acquisition device (LAD). He told us that babies are born with an innate language learning potential and their brains are programmed and ready for communication. **Chomsky** found that children not only learn words when they begin to talk but also how to put words together and in the right order – they are learning 'grammar'.

He found that many sentences we use have a deep structure with more than one surface structure, for example:

◆ George caught a fish today.

◆ A fish was caught by George today.

◆ It was a fish that George caught.

◆ What George caught was a fish.

How *do* children learn this? You will possibly agree that it is very complicated! Different languages such as Chinese, Swahili and English have these deep structures and so **Chomsky** proposed that there is an innate awareness of deep structures universally. He told us that children have the ability to learn complex grammar, referring to them as

Noam Chomsky (1928–)

'intuitive grammarians'. So if we return to the sentences used by John earlier, we can see that children apply the same rules – 'hurted' because it was in the past tense – and whilst practising grammar the child is using the past tense without exception. **Chomsky** told us that children did not learn this grammar by sitting down and being taught but by listening to all the linguistic evidence they hear around them.

THINK ABOUT IT

Try to think of some examples in your practice of children doing the following:

◆ imitating speech of an adult

◆ using a deep structure sentence with more than one surface structure

◆ LAD – the child is applying a knowledge they could not have imitated or copied from an adult.

You might also want to look at some studies of children deprived of human contact: for example, the 'Wild Boy of Averyon', a boy found in a forest all alone in 1799 – links can be found for this and other similar cases at www.FeralChildren.com.

The semantic approach

After **Chomsky**'s findings, others began to look at the process of language acquisition to try to find out how important cognitive and social factors were in the process. In the late 1960s, systematic investigations began to look at how children might be attempting to make sense of the world around them and be seen as meaning makers.

In 1970, **Lois Bloom** conducted a piece of research in which she made 'rich interpretations of the intended meanings of young children'. She showed examples of children using language – often just the same two words to convey different meanings. **Bloom** gives the following example:

Kathryn, aged 21 months, used the words 'mummy sock' twice in the same day but in two different contexts. The first time was when Kathryn picked up her mother's sock and said 'mummy sock' ('this sock belongs to mummy'). The second time was when her mother was dressing her and she said 'mummy sock' ('mummy is putting my sock on me').

THINK ABOUT IT

Think of some examples of young children using two words over again to mean something different, for example 'big cat' meaning 'I want the big cat' and 'look at the big cat'.

Some of these findings suggested that cognitive development precedes language development. These raised many questions and further debate about the relationship between language and thought. For example:

- Does a child require the concept (idea) of an object or an action before learning the correct word for that object or action?
- Does knowing the word for an object or an action help the child understand and develop the concept of it?

THINK ABOUT IT

Do you have any answers to these two questions? It is a difficult idea to unpick! You might try looking at the ideas of **Vygotsky**, **Bruner**, **Piaget** and, more recently, **Steven Pinker** to untangle the puzzle of the relationship between thought and language. (There are books in the References at the end of this chapter which you can refer to, such as **Vygotsky**'s *Thought and Language* and **Marian Whitehead**'s book.)

Piaget and **Vygotsky** also had views on the relationship between language and thought which are summarised in the table below.

The relationship between language and thought: Piaget and Vygotsky

Piaget	Vygotsky
Piaget believed that language was only one of the possible ways in which children represented their knowledge. He was sure that thought preceded language and that therefore the language children use represents their cognitive development. He believed that language is a symbolic system used to represent our experiences.	Vygotsky said that although thought and language occurred together, they did not necessarily have the same beginnings. He told us that thinking is a cognitive activity and will take place as children learn more about their world. Language develops because the child hears it from the adults and other children around them. He told us that, at around 2 years of age, pre-linguistic thought and intellectual language join together and that it then has two functions for the child: - internal function: to direct thought - external social function: to communicate with other people.

Margaret Donaldson also found that language development is dependent on children's more general cognitive development. She gave examples of the way in which children can grasp meaning and make sense of situations, including the following example:

An English woman is in the company of an Arab woman and her two children, a boy of 7 and a little girl of 13 months who is just beginning to walk but is afraid to take more than a few steps without help. The English woman speaks no Arabic, the Arab woman and her son speak no English.

The little girl walks to the English woman and back to her mother. Then she turns as if to start off in the direction of the English woman again. But the latter now smiles, points to the boy and says 'Walk to your brother this time'. At once the boy understands the situation, although he understands not a word of the language, and holds out his arms. The baby smiles, changes direction and walks to her brother. Like the older child, she appears to understand the situation perfectly.

Source: Donaldson (1978), page 37

THINK ABOUT IT

Consider **Donaldson**'s example above.

◆ How do you think the children are able to understand what the English woman is saying to them?

◆ Is this very human situation able to tell the children something without words being necessary?

The semantic perspective demonstrates children's ability to make sense of the world and human situations. Children are not just passive 'empty vessels', as the behaviourists suggest, nor are they just born with an innate ability to learn language, as the nativists suggest.

The interactionist approach

This approach looks at the part the adult plays in the child's language development. Although these theories recognise the biological and environmental factors as important, both **Jerome Bruner** and **Michael Halliday** (quoted in Maynard and Thomas (2004), page 35) state that babies can understand the function of language before they are able to produce words themselves. You will be able to see this when observing a very young baby and their carer. **Catherine Snow** called this 'conversation-like exchanges'. There is a special and simpler language parents use when talking to their baby – first termed as 'motherese' and more recently called 'parentese'. Parents want to communicate with the baby and need to understand the baby's needs. They do this by using eye-to-eye contact, repetition and turn-taking and will say that they understand what the baby is trying to tell them. **Bruner** says that this special language provides the child with a language acquisition support system (LASS).

This very young baby shares a special language with her father

THINK ABOUT IT

Think about times when you have observed a parent using LASS – this may have been at mealtime, bedtime, playtime or bath time.

- Did the parent use a particular language or code to help the child?
- How did the baby react?
- Did the baby attempt to imitate the parent?

We will be discussing these very early interactions in further detail later in the chapter.

Summary of the key theories on language acquisition

Theory	Theorist	Emphasis
Behaviourist	B.F. Skinner	On language being learned through imitation – and being nurtured by the parent
Nativist	Noam Chomsky	On innate ability – nature – the child's ability to understand language and the complexities of grammar
Semantic	Lois Bloom Mary Donaldson	On the link between cognitive and language development
Interactionist	Jerome Bruner Michael Halliday	On the interaction between infant and adult – both social/communicative parts of language development

The importance of early social interaction

From non-verbal to verbal communication

H.R. Schaffer (2004) tells us that the very earliest interactions with the primary care-givers are essential in supporting the development of language in young children. Babies respond well to the parents' use of 'motherese' or 'parentese' speech (see the examples in the table below).

Schaffer's examples of how parentese is used

Characteristics	Some features of speech used by the adult
Phonological	Very clear enunciation Higher pitched voice Exaggerated intonation Slower way of speaking Long pauses to wait for response from baby
Syntactic	Shorter pieces of speech or length of talking Sentences well formed and spoken Less complexity in sentences
Semantic	'Baby talk' words Limited range of vocabulary Always referring to what is happening in the present
Pragmatic	More clear directions More questions Repetition of the child's sounds Strategies to get the baby's attention

Source: Adapted from Schaffer (2004), page 125

You will have heard adults using 'parentese' when interacting with their children. There can be no doubt that this support and encouragement can help to make the acquisition of language meaningful and enjoyable for the child. However, it has not been proven without doubt that this is necessary for children to acquire speech. This is because research carried out across cultures shows that not all cultures adopt a 'parentese' language style and this does not seem to prevent their children from learning language later. For example, the Kalui of Papua New Guinea rarely engage with their babies in this way and treat them as if they have absolutely no understanding, using a very directive style of speaking to the child as they get older. However, these children become users of language within the normal time, because they were still listening and watching the adults.

Children, it would seem, are very determined to communicate with others and have an innate ability to do so even if they are hampered by a hearing impairment.

Marian Whitehead (1999) tells us that young children are 'great communicators'. She says that, in these earliest communications, babies learn a great deal about themselves and how others see them. The responses of their carers show them how lovable and unique they are. **Whitehead** tells us that through these early interactions young babies learn a way of life. She tells us that the main characteristics of non-verbal communication are:

◆ face-to-face intimacy

◆ a range of strong feelings – warmth, rage, frustration

◆ whole body movements – dancing, gestures, head shaking and nodding, waving, etc.

◆ mouth sounds – whistles, humming, blowing raspberries, boos and coos.

Whitehead also tells us that first words are not just random sounds and can be identified in the following way:

◆ They are suddenly used by the child.

◆ They are used regularly during the same activity or environment.

◆ The carer knows what they mean.

Consider the following case study.

CASE STUDY:

FIRST WORDS

Katy has begun to use a lot of words over the last few months. Her parents have noted that after they have put her to bed they can hear her on the baby monitor 'talking away to herself' for quite a while before she falls to sleep. She repeats the names of her family, she talks about the things she has done that day and parts of her body.

What do you think Katy is doing before she falls asleep?

You might have considered that Katy is in fact practising all the words she knows, repeating them to herself so that she can remember them and get them right.

Whitehead explains that language is power to children because it enables them to explain themselves and show that they are also thinking for themselves. It is evident that children learn a great deal more than just words and that they also grasp quite complex grammar in a short period of time. **Whitehead** explains rules of language in the following way:

◆ phonology – organisation and pattern of sounds

◆ syntax – a meaningful combination of words

◆ semantics – groups of words and their meanings.

GOOD PRACTICE CHECKLIST

Supporting very young children's communication

- Pay close attention to children so that you can help them make sense of the world and their part in it.
- Use plenty of play talk and interaction with parents, family, siblings, extended family, key workers, practitioners and other babies.
- Provide a suitable environment – small cosy rooms, blankets and floor cushions, full length curtains to hide behind, trees, bushes and peep-holes and hiding places.
- Provide activities such as face-to-face gazing, singing, dancing, clapping, talking, bouncing; plenty of opportunities for listening and watching, quiet times; mobiles and treasure baskets (see Chapter 6), musical instruments, played music, saucepan lids and rattles – anything that makes an interesting sound!
- Provide relaxed opportunities for talking within the routine – quiet one-to-one time to support the development of complex ideas.

THINK ABOUT IT

Using the good practice checklist above, complete the table below by including ways in which you might support each age and stage of language development. Some examples have been included.

Supporting language development

Age	Typical language ability	How will you support language development?
6 months	Turns to mother's voice across room Responds to name Vocalises tunefully Laughs and squeals aloud when playing Responds to angry or friendly tones in the adult voice	*Example: provide stimulus through lots of face-to-face gazing*
1 year	Chatters loudly and frequently Is able to show that they understand several words in context Understands simple instructions – especially if the adult gives vocal cues Imitates adult's vocalisations – and this may often sound like a word Will hand an object to an adult on request, for example a spoon – shows definition by use	*Example: giving the child the opportunity to practise words – with visual cues such as pictures in a supermarket*

18 months	Chatters loudly to themselves at play Uses conversational tones and emotional inflections Uses 6–20 recognisable words and understands many more Enjoys nursery rhymes and tries to join in Obeys simple commands	*Example: ensure that the child has opportunities for singing nursery rhymes and word play*
2 years	Uses 50 or more recognisable words and can understand more Begins to listen with interest to general conversation Can use predispositions – such as 'in', 'under', 'or', 'on' Constantly asking names of objects and people 'Mine' and 'me' are beginning to emerge Responds to simple questions	*Example: hide and seek and games which include very simple instructions*
3 years	Uses pronouns 'I', 'you', 'me' correctly Can use three-word sentences Verbs begin to be in the majority Knows parts of the body Has around 900–1000 words Understands simple questions dealing with their own environment Asks more questions beginning with 'what' 'where' and 'who' Still talks to self in long monologues especially during fantasy play Should be able to tell you their age, sex and name Knows several nursery rhymes	*Example: songs such as 'Head, shoulders, knees and toes'; questions such as 'Who did you go to see yesterday?'*
4 years	Knows names of familiar animals Names common objects in books Knows one or more colours Speech is grammatically correct and can be understood Listens to and tells long stories Can count by rote up to 20 or more Uses extensive verbalisation when playing Knows several nursery rhymes and songs which they can sing correctly	*Example: use of favourite story books – ask the child to retell stories or 'play out' a particular familiar plot*

5 years	Fluent use of speech Can repeat sentences as long as nine words Should be able to follow three commands Knows own age Loves to read or tell stories and can also act them out Enjoys jokes and riddles Understands tomorrow, yesterday and today Can use long and complex sentences	*Example: encourage child to collect things to help them retell stories and experiences*
6 years	Speech should now be completely intelligible and socially useful Should have mastered f, v, sh, zh, th Should understand concepts up to 7 Should be able to tell a story about a picture and see relationships between objects and happenings	*Example: give the child opportunity to plan a particular task – and consider all factors – i.e plan an activity with friends*
7 years	Should have mastered the consonants s/z, r, voiceless th, ch, wh, and the soft g Understands terms such as 'alike', 'different', 'beginning', 'end' Should be beginning to be able to tell the time Simple reading and write many words	*Example: read a story and give the child opportunity to compose a song or write a story based in their own experiences*
8 years	All speech sounds including consonant blends should be clear and established Should be reading with ease Be able to carry on conversation with an adult Has developed time and number concepts Few grammatical mistakes should be made	*Example: opportunities for presenting ideas to a group*

Tina Bruce (see Chapter 2) carried out research between 1999 and 2003 in the Castelbrea Community Cluster, which is part of the Craigmillar area in Edinburgh. The results of this research were discussed in her book, *Developing Learning in Early Childhood*. One of the key themes of this book was communication. She tells us that communication is about first 'getting in touch with ourselves' and then getting in touch with others. **Bruce** explains that when there is good communication between parents, children and practitioners in a setting, good quality learning takes place. She also tells us that interaction with others is central to the language development of young children. **Bruce** supports an interactionist approach for practitioners wanting to find effective ways of communicating with children. This can be achieved by sharing experiences with children and using all mediums of communication to do this, for example looking at photographs, visits, play scenarios. Non-verbal communication is 85 per cent of all our communication with others. We can communicate without using words but we cannot communicate without using our bodies.

CASE STUDY:

SAHIRA'S HEDGEHOG

Paul is supporting Sahira with an activity. Sahira has produced a wonderful model in clay and is very proud of it. Paul has encouraged her to keep going with the piece of work when she found it difficult. He bends down next to her and comments on the lovely shape of her model and the wonderful detail she has put into it by using other implements. Sahira tells him that her model is a hedgehog. Paul continues by asking Sahira where she would like to keep the model. He stays beside her while she puts it on a shelf in the classroom, advising her that this shelf is possibly a good idea as her Mum will see it immediately when she come to pick her up from nursery.

1 How is Paul supporting Sahira's language development?

2 What sort of non-verbal communication is he using here to demonstrate to Sahira that he values her work?

3 How have Sahira and Paul exchanged information?

Children communicating through dance

Bruce tells us that we can communicate non-verbally in two ways:

◆ through our bodies – voices and facial expressions

◆ through a variety of art forms – music, dance, visual arts.

These mediums can be used to support learning language or as a substitute form of communication. When we communicate, different parts of the brain need to work co-operatively making everything happen at once. **Bruce** tells us that children are constantly trying to ascertain several things at once:

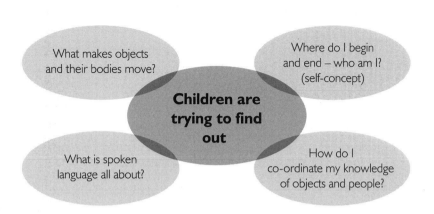

Children are investigating lots of things all at once!

Bruce tells us that the group of researchers who look at this co-ordination of the brain are called 'connectionists'. **Gopnik** *et al.* (1999) claim that babies are 'citizens of the world' as they start life being able to discriminate between the different sounds of languages. However, he tells us that later the brain alters and the child begins to hear sounds differently so they can no longer discriminate between different languages. **Gopnik** also says that 'learning a language is about co-ordinating what you do with what other people do' and that adults can support children to learn language through a loving and supportive atmosphere. Consider the following overview of the ways in which **Bruce** suggests we might support language.

Supporting language development: applying Bruce's theories to practice

Good practice in creating the right environment and relationships for language development	How to ensure that this happens
The right kind of atmosphere	◆ Use the right tone of voice and body language – speaking quietly and calmly, getting down to the child's level ◆ Warmth and encouragement – the way we look at children will let them know whether or not we support them or are critical of them
Developing memory skills	◆ Maintain opportunities for discussion about places, facts, events and people (semantic memory) ◆ Exercises and activities to practise recall (episodic memory) ◆ Teach by showing and doing, doing something repeatedly in order to remember it (procedural memory)

Develop good conversations with children	◆ Support children to find ways forward and find solutions for problems ◆ Develop and deepen thoughts through discussion of ideas ◆ Observe and tune-in to non-verbal communication sensitively ◆ Support children to feel confident to try out new words and ideas without fear of ridicule
Plenty of sleep and rest	Ensure that children have plenty of opportunities for sleep and restful periods during the day
Opportunities for children to express thoughts and feelings through language	◆ Ensure that children know they matter and that their views and ideas are valued ◆ Listen to children and when speaking use an appropriate tone of voice ◆ Encourage the children to talk to each other about their feelings and take turns in sharing their experiences
Sharing thoughts and ideas with others	◆ Give children opportunities to work together with the support of the adult to sustain periods of shared thinking ◆ Give children opportunities to work alongside an adult where they can discuss their thoughts in a non-threatening situation

Supporting children in early literacy

In this section, we will look at how adults can support children in becoming literate. This is quite a complex process and in order to do this we will consider:

◆ some of the present frameworks used to support early language

◆ contextualisation of language development

◆ ways to observe language development

◆ using symbols

◆ the role of books and stories in developing language

◆ encouraging early writing skills

◆ encouraging early reading skills

◆ supporting children for whom English is an additional language

◆ dyslexia.

Some of the present frameworks used to support early language

Supporting children to become literate is something we do from the moment a baby is born. Although we are clearly not expecting a baby to write their own stories, we are working to underpin this vital part of their development. In the Birth to Three Matters Framework pack (see Chapter 1, page 11), the pink cards tell us that the four components of 'A skilful communicator' are:

- being together – becoming sociable and effective communicators and developing positive relationships
- finding a voice – becoming competent and confident users of language
- listening and responding – listening and responding to others appropriately
- making meaning – communicating meaning and influencing others, negotiating and making choices.

TRY IT OUT

We have already looked at suggestions for good practice in these areas. In your setting, look at the ways in which you feel the children are meeting the outcomes of the Birth to Three Matters Framework. Observe a young child doing one of the following:
- *being together*
- *finding a voice*
- *listening and responding to an adult or another child*
- *making meaning.*

When you have done this, evaluate whether you feel this was an opportunity for the child to become literate.

You will probably have found lots of examples of these sorts of interaction. You may have found it slightly more difficult to link it directly to the child's ability to become literate. This is because so much of development of literacy skills is subliminal.

The Curriculum Guidance for the Foundation Stage (see Chapter 1, page 2) tells us that children should have the opportunity to be involved in:

- interaction with others – negotiation and taking turns
- listening with enjoyment to spoken and written language
- sustained attentive listening
- listening with enjoyment and responding to stories – making up own songs, stories and rhymes
- extending their vocabulary – exploring meaning and sounds of new words
- speaking clearly and audibly with confidence
- using language to imagine and recreate roles and experiences
- using talk to organise, sequence and clarify thinking.

Contextualisation of language development

Michael Halliday (cited in Riley, 2003, page 62) claimed that he found through his research that there is classification of different functions of language:

1 Speak in order 'to get things done'.
2 Control the behaviour of others.
3 Interact so that we might establish relationships with others.

We have already looked at ways in which **Bruce** suggests we can do this.

Jenni Riley and David Reedy tell us that children gradually begin to express their needs and their thoughts more fluently as they get older. The use of language helps the child to organise their thoughts and categorise them if necessary. They tell us that language has both a contextualised and decontextualised use, shown in the diagram below.

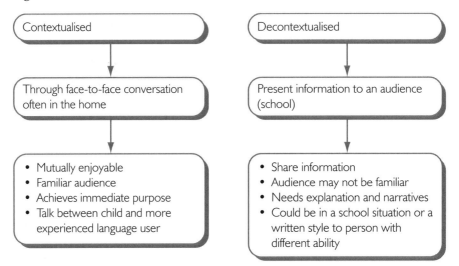

Contextualised and decontextualised use of language

Of course, it is clear to see that the decontextualised skills are likely to be present in an older child and one that has had a lot of experience and practice at explaining things to others. The contextualised use is easier for young children who are more confident on a one-to-one basis and have built trusting relationships.

Ways to observe language development

We can observe children in order to look at the ways in which they are communicating using any one of the following methods:

◆ written narrative – not always easy to get all speech written down

◆ event samples – especially useful when a child is in a new situation

◆ time samples – can be used to record the talk taking place throughout the day

◆ checklists – can be useful to record specific areas of language development, i.e. use of scientific language (see the example below)

◆ audio recording – recording children speaking can be very effective but beware of background noise!

◆ video recording – this is also useful as it can record shared conversations and the verbal and non-verbal language that takes place

◆ examples of children's writing, drawing and mark-making.

Observation		
Name:	Alicia	
Age:	3 years 7 months	
Date:	5 June 200–	
Time:	10am	
People present:	Practitioner and observer and two other children	

Task:	Writing a story	Comment
Follows instruction		Alicia was keen to give ideas, but did not listen well to the adult when she gave instructions.
Interaction with adult/other children		Alicia was distracted and did not maintain eye-contact with the adult. She did not answer questions from the other children, although she was smiling and attempted to hold Sarah's hand.
Ability to concentrate on task (give time)		When the adult asked the children to do a drawing of their story ideas (these had been discussed), Alicia began enthusiastically but after 4 mins she was distracted and wanted to leave the group.
Participation in conversation		Alicia did not turn-take during the conversation. She wanted the adult to listen to her first and seemed to be distracted by playing with Sarah's hair.

Example checklist observation

THINK ABOUT IT

In the example checklist observation above, Alicia has some problems with following instructions and listening skills and the early years practitioner wants to observe her to see how much she needs to develop.

What would you do after having completed this checklist observation?

Using symbols

If children are given the right opportunities, they find ways of holding on to experiences they have had and can represent them to others. They can do this through a variety of representations:

◆ dance – making up their own dances

◆ music – making up songs and tunes

◆ art – woodwork, sewing, clay, paintings.

Also through the written word – information, stories, rhymes:

◆ by being read to – accessing information about other ideas, hearing other people's stories

◆ music – writing down symbols so that we can remember the music.

Abraham Maslow said that:

'If you deliberately plan to be less than you are capable of being, then I warn you that you will be deeply unhappy for the rest of your life. You will be evading your possibilities.'

Source: Maslow (1987), page 40

It is really important to support and encourage children to 'make personal symbols' (Bruce, 2004). **Bruce** explains that if you take the children's interests as a starting point you will help them to stretch their capabilities and reach their individual potential. The case study below is an example from practice.

CASE STUDY:

JOE AND THE DECORATING

Joe is 4 years old. He has recently moved house after a long wait to move. His mother and his older sister are very excited about the move as it means they will all have their own bedrooms. In their last flat, they all shared a bedroom. On Joe's first day back to nursery he brings photos of his new bedroom and the house to share with the other children. He articulately describes all the rooms in the house to them at length. He tells the nursery teacher that he is going to help his mum decorate.

Over the next week, Joe uses every opportunity he is given to make plans for his bedroom. First with the large blocks – placing one as his bed and two as his wardrobe in a layout on the floor. At story time he asks for the storybook *Moving House* to be read. Whilst playing imaginatively with his friends, he organises them to carry the paint back from the shops and help him make up the wallpaper paste in a bucket. He carefully organises things in the corner of the post office telling the other children they will have to leave now as it 'could get a bit mucky in here'!

The teacher has a chat with Joe and asks him what he would like to do in nursery about his decorating. Joe suggests that the wall in the post office corner needs decorating. The teacher provides an opportunity for Joe and his friends to wallpaper the wall behind the post office shop.

This case study shows an example of a child-led activity that is rich in opportunites for language development and use of symbols.

What ways could the staff make use of this opportunity to support the children's language development?

Bruce explains that the use of symbols can be productive for the children and practitioners. In the case study above, photographs were taken by the staff so that the children could look back at the event (episodic memory) and discuss how they decorated the post office and the skills that they used (procedural memory). The photographs were left in easy reach so that the children could take them home and talk to their families about their work and also discuss them with each other on a daily basis.

Bruce suggests some of the following ideas for good practice.

GOOD PRACTICE CHECKLIST

Creating an environment that encourages children to become symbol users

◆ The book corner should be warm, cosy and well lit. Books should include books made by staff and children. Provide cushions to sit and lay and an adult-sized sofa for children to share books with adults and each other.

◆ Put labels on equipment – words with a picture on drawers, cupboards and doors, arrows to show directions to get to places, for example:
'This way to the post office ⇨'.

◆ Display children's work in its entirety and original form (not cut up to become part of something the practitioner has invented).

◆ Use labels and signs made by the children, for example 'Joe's decorating team' written by Joe and his team.

◆ Use real-life symbols, for example a picture of a child putting on his or her coat on the door to the cloakroom.

◆ Position symbols and signs at the children's height.

It is important that children feel relaxed whilst sharing a book together

The role of books and stories in developing language

Bruner claimed that children learn a great deal about the cultural world by reading stories. He believed that children used narratives to help them understand their own experiences and communicate to other people what their experiences might be. **Schaffer** also tells us that it is important for young children to be involved in 'pre-reading' skills to be ready for reading. These skills will include:

- repetition
- perception
- understanding of reading conventions (stories in books, reading from left to right, etc.)
- awareness of rhyming
- concept of story.

Schaffer suggests that when children learn to read they will need to consider visual information as well as the sound and sense of words. Training for these skills will have already been given in the form of picture-matching games, jigsaws and exercises in grading shapes.

Early years settings use illustrated picture books that help the children to interact with each other to bring the text alive. A useful storybook for these earliest literacy experiences is *We're Going on a Bear Hunt* by Michael Rosen, which has all the essential ingredients for early interaction and reading skills:

- opportunities for the children to relate to the characters in the story as they are referred to as 'we'
- opportunities to join in with the story and quickly learn to know what is coming next
- plenty of repetition and opportunities for the children to speculate about what might happen next
- valuable lessons about the phonic system with words such as 'deep dark forest' and 'swishy swashy'
- opportunities to discuss being frightened and the security of home
- the chance to enter the world of anticipation and excitement when they want and leave it if they want.

You can use this story to ask the children questions:

- How does it make you feel?
- Is the bear lonely?
- How far is it before they get home?

Very young children therefore enjoy and benefit from stories that have the following:

- familiar objects and people
- repetition of language and sentences, such as 'Where is he?', 'Is he here?' at the end of every page
- a story which makes them feel things
- a short story with less than 25 words on a page (of course this will change as the child gets older)
- patterns in the story – so that the child might guess what will happen next.

The story illustrated above has familiar objects for a young child that may already be part of their experience or knowledge. It has repetition so that the child will learn to join in with the story. It also has a pattern to the story so that the child can guess what will happen next. These sorts of stories give the adult the opportunity to talk to the child and extend and support their language development.

Clay (1979) believed that talking to children is one of the most effective ways to develop their spoken language. She suggests that adults should:

◆ listen when a child wants to talk to you

◆ talk to the child who is less likely to initiate a conversation with you

◆ reply to all questions and extend conversation whenever possible

◆ take note that the children who are good talkers will talk the most – adults will need to identify those children and identify those who do not talk so that they can spend more time with them.

THINK ABOUT IT

◆ Think about a child in your setting who talks a lot and is confident in speaking up. Observe how much time you spend talking to that child in one day.

◆ Think about a child who hardly ever speaks to you. Observe how much time you spend talking to that child in one day.

You may be surprised at the amounts of time you spend actually talking to either of these children. In a busy working day with so much to do practitioners often find it difficult to make time to speak to every child. A way to improve on this is to plan more small-group activities that give opportunities for discussion with the adult involved.

Encouraging early writing skills

Whitehead (1999) discusses in detail supporting early language and literacy skills for children. She suggested that the earliest experiences of sharing books with babies helped children with their love of books in later life. Whitehead also talked about the optimum literacy conditions for young children. This is when children are saturated with print in their everyday lives. An interest in print will ensure that they can become more efficient mark-makers and writers. She says that print should be:

◆ everyday print that we find all around us – on our clothes, television, computers, shops, restaurants, letters from relatives, visits to places of worship, the post office and supermarkets – print is just about everywhere

◆ print for pleasure – songs, chants, rhymes, poetry, dances – any opportunity for a child to exploit and play around with words

◆ print for investigation – opportunities to develop their own alphabets, labelling, making lists, school registers – lists of words that start with the same sound, people and places.

When children are surrounded by lots of print and given opportunities to use it in meaningful ways, they become confident in using writing or symbols to tell other people what they know.

CASE STUDY:

CATHY AND THE SCHOOLROOM

Cathy was 5 years old. She and her sister often played for hours writing names of pupils for the register they kept on the 'teacher's desk', collecting details such as age and name and address from other imaginary children – all details that could be added to the 'register' in the schoolroom. Cathy and her sister looked keenly in the books of their dolls and 'tutted' and 'nodded' whilst they 'marked' the schoolbooks. When the school bell rang they would sit for a while and make plans for the school play.

1 Cathy and her sister were playing imaginatively. What early literacy skills were they practising?

2 How was imitation helping them to become confident writers?

You will have many examples of children using the everyday examples of print around them to practise their writing skills. They will invent library systems and shops with price tags, banks will be recreated to offer them opportunity to 'write cheques' and 'stamp' receipts. **Whitehead** also talks about 'young writers' strategies' (see the table below):

The strategies of young writers

Strategy	What the young writer does
Asking questions	Children will directly ask us what print means, they will also ask us how they should write it.
Watching others	Children will watch others – especially adults or older siblings – and imitate the way in which they write – imitating all sorts of mannerisms such as sucking the pencil.
Using names	Children will use their names to help them as they will probably write their name fairly early on in their writing career. They will especially use the ends of names and their combinations such as 'er' or 'ia'.
Exploiting knowledge	Children will create messages and stories using only the letters and names they know – filling in the rest with kisses (xxxxx), repeated words or heart shapes.
Using alphabets or sounds	Children will play with alphabets and sounds. They may write only the consonants, for example 'tbl' instead of 'table'. They will also invent codes.
Scribble	Scribble is very important as it shows that the child understands that writing is not the same as drawing. It is often written in lines and is nearly always written quickly – just like a confident writer!
Lists and inventories	Just as in the case study, children will write well-organised lists in horizontal and vertical lines. Later this will become a way of writing what they know and then for checking and organising.
Words and pictures	When children draw a picture and write words underneath, they are demonstrating a knowledge that pictures and writing together tell a story.

Encouraging early reading skills

Since the introduction of the National Literacy Strategy in 1998, there has been significant improvement in attainment in reading English at every key stage. The National Strategies aim to provide teachers with the right kinds of resources and teaching methods to ensure that standards in the UK improve. The essential elements of this approach are to ensure that:

◆ there is a clear focus to improve achievement

◆ teachers in all schools have easy access to the best methodologies for teaching reading and are trained to use them effectively

◆ there is early emphasis on phonics with complementary reading strategies

◆ teaching is tailored effectively to the needs of individual children and children with particular needs are given the right kind of support

- there are appropriate programmes in place for younger children which develop their communication and literacy skills through play
- parents are encouraged to support children to learn to read and to enjoy reading.

Source: Adapted from DfES (2005)

In the early years setting, this encouragement for early reading skills can also be enhanced by good practice in planning for the essential components of early reading skills:

- name recognition – ensuring that every child has the opportunity to see their name written, for example on coat pegs, at snack time; at the writing table; at every activity. This early recognition can also be supported by using coloured cards for names – so that the child also recognises the colour as well as the shape of their name
- opportunities for rhyming – practising sounds through listening to tape recordings and poems and encouraging the children to join in with rhyming words
- picture lotto and sound lotto – pictures with the word to be matched are useful as well as taped sounds with word cards
- story corner – obviously central to encouraging children's appreciation of the written word – a rich variety of books including poetry, stories, information, traditional tales, pop-up books, dual language books, counting books, children's cookery books
- pictures with words throughout the nursery setting where they can be seen by the child
- tracking of the way the words are read by pointing from left to right whilst reading the story.

Phonics

In the early years, it is essential that children develop phonological (sounds) and graphical (sight) awareness. In the mid-twentieth century, the alphabetical method of learning to read (seeing, hearing letter sounds and words) was challenged by the use of phonics (Grahame and Kelly, 2000).

Phonics is about working with sounds and decoding those sounds as opposed to using the names of the letters to read. The simplest way to explain this use of sounds is to look at the word 'cat'. We would need to break this up into three sounds, C – A –T, and when we want the child to write the word they would hear the three sounds and represent them with the appropriate letters. When children are first introduced to phonics, they are taught to hear and identify individual vowel and consonant sounds (phonemes) and recognise the symbols used for these sounds (graphemes). However, as the English language is not phonically regular (not everything is spelt the way it sounds), this is made a little difficult and the rules do not apply to all words. **Grahame and Kelly** tell us that there are 26 letters in our alphabet to represent 44 sounds.

> **TRY IT OUT**
>
> *Think of some words that cannot be spelt phonically, for example 'any', 'phone', 'without'. Can you think of any more?*

Children therefore have to also learn and take on board that some letters 'double count' (Graham and Kelly, 2000, page 12). For example, the letter 's' in 'soft' makes a different sound in 'was'. Some sounds are represented by combining letters, for example 'sh' in 'shop'. There are three phonemes: 'sh'–'o'–'p' and the written representation is with four letters: 's'–'h'–'o'–'p'. In spite of these difficulties, the use of phonics is a requirement of the National Curriculum. At present many settings and schools adopt a combination of:

◆ *analytical phonics* This approach is to analyse chunks of words and encourage detecting these patterns across all words. The children analyse letter sounds and teaching starts at whole word level. Children are usually taught one letter sound per week and are then shown pictures and words starting with that sound, moving onto letter sounds in the middle of the word to sound and blend the consecutive letters, for example: 'cuh' – 'ah' – 'tuh' for CAT.

◆ *synthetic phonics* The phonemes are isolated in the word and then they are blended together to help decode the word. Children listen to the spoken word, select the letters and place them together (they may use magnetic letters to do this), sounding out the sounds and blending them to produce the word. The advantages of this system are that children are taught a process to apply when they meet an unfamiliar word. One example of this is from Hickey's multi-sensory language course (Angur and Briggs, 1992) – from the first six letter sounds (s a t i p n) the children will make up three-letter words ('sat', 'pin', 'tin').

> **THINK ABOUT IT**
>
> To research the subject of phonics and the advantages of its use, you might want to look at the Rose Review (2005), written by Jim Rose, a former Ofsted inspector, at www.standards.dfes.gov.uk/rosereview/interim. This is an independent review into the teaching of early reading including the role played by synthetic phonics.

In the early years setting, **Graham and Kelly** tell us that we can support children to be sensitive to sound and encourage them to promote their ability to listen generally. They suggest the following:

- Sound walks – taking children out and asking them to focus on the sounds around them – traffic, birds, aeroplanes overhead.

- Guess the name of the instrument – placed in a bag or on a sound tape, ask the children to guess the name of the instrument by listening to the sound it makes.

- Voice play – playing with sounds such as 'ooooohhh!', 'ahhhh!' or 'shhhh!' – children will learn these later as phonemes.

- Rhymes and rhythm – offer children the opportunity to practise these as much as possible – nursery rhymes; singing; dancing games – give the children opportunity to guess the next word or phrase in a song.

- Odd one out – use words that rhyme: 'say', 'hay', 'gay', 'may' and add one that does not rhyme – the children need to indicate when that happens.

- Alphabet letters – opportunities for children to become familiar with alphabet letters – through songs, books and magnetic letters.

Source: Adapted from Grahame and Kelly, 2000, page 89

We have considered a very brief overview of phonics. There is a plethora of information available on the subject of phonics and it will always be at the centre of the UK government's agenda for improving standards in schools. You will almost certainly need to explore the subject further to meet the needs of your job role. You will need to have knowledge of ways in which children can be supported in the early years so that they have a keen awareness of sound and graphics.

Supporting children for whom English is an additional language

Jenni Riley and David Reedy confirm that there are two conditions which need to occur for effective learning of a second language. These are:

- The second language needs to be developed from the basis of a well established and maintained first language.

- The first language should be respected and encouraged.

They also tell us that the practitioners working with children should have a positive attitude. There should be a positive and enabling atmosphere, which the practitioner will need to follow.

GOOD PRACTICE CHECKLIST

Supporting a child in developing an additional language

- Establish what the child can do through observation and assessment.
- Plan for the next stage of learning.
- Integrate language support into the setting so that it is meaningful.
- Support the child to feel secure in the setting.
- Ensure that they know their first language is valued.
- Promote the first language positively – invite friends or relatives of the child in to interpret for key events.
- Translate class-made books and favourite stories into dual texts.
- Use drama, finger puppets and story boards to encourage visual learning of the language.
- Ask a family member to read a story to the other children in the first language so that they have some understanding of the risk the child is taking in learning the new language.
- Include the child in all class activities.
- Use sorting and matching activities.

In the earliest stages of their learning a new language, **Riley and Reedy** tell us that:

- there will be a period of silence where communication will occur through gesture and non-verbal communication
- the child will gradually begin to put two words together in order to express themselves – 'me too' or 'go away'.

It can take up to two years for a child to become fluent in an additional language and this may only be in supported situations. It may take longer to use the language accurately.

Dyslexia

Dyslexia is one of the most common challenges faced by children, with an estimated incidence rate of 5 per cent in the western world. The World Federation of Neurology (1996) defined dyslexia as:

'A disorder in children who, despite conventional classroom experience, fail to attain the language skills of reading, writing and spelling commensurate with their intellectual abilities.'

Source: www.nfneurology.org./wfn

This definition seems a very negative definition and it would probably be a little disturbing to the parent of a child with dyslexia.

It is likely that you have at some time dealt with a dyslexic child (or will do in the future) or that in fact you may even be dyslexic yourself. So it is vital that we consider some of the possible reasons for dyslexia and the effects it can have on a child's learning.

The word 'dyslexic' comes from the Greek words *dys* (difficulty with) and *lexis* (words). Children are most often identified at school as being dyslexic when they find reading a challenge or even earlier if they have problems playing with words and rhymes. The table below shows some of the characteristics of dyslexia and how they might affect learning.

Characteristics of dyslexia

Characteristic	How is the child's learning affected?
Phonological difficulty	The child has difficulty breaking words down. They can also have challenges taking sounds and linking them to a word.
Limited visual recall	Some dyslexic children have poor visual memories and are therefore unable to recall a word. Spelling and handwriting can also be a challenge.
Sequencing	Children will often get numbers and words in the wrong order and have problems knowing the difference between left and right, which can be confusing.
Language processes	Some children with dyslexia have difficulties in this area – they may find it difficult to answer questions particularly if time is involved.
Orientation	Spatial relationships are a challenge and some children have an inability to distinguish left or right, leaving them totally confused.

Nicholson and Fawcett (1990) claim that the key to dyslexia is that there seems to have been early problems in articulation. They suggest that when the child was younger they would have had problems with repeating words correctly. The characteristics mentioned in the table above mean that the child has difficulty with phonics.

However, it is not always as extreme as this and will vary from child to child.

THINK ABOUT IT

Your setting will have strategies to support the child. What strategies do you know for supporting a child with dyslexia?

You may want to do some further research and can find out more from the Dyslexia Institute (www.dyslexiainst.org.uk).

Summary

In this chapter we have considered how children learn to speak through looking first at some of the theoretical perspectives: behaviourist; nativist; semantic; and interactionist. We have taken on board some of the ideas of **Vygotsky** and **Piaget** on the acquisition of language. We have found that children acquire language through a complex group of factors: an innate ability to learn language (LAD) and the support of the adult for imitation and secure conversations from an early age (LASS). **Bruce** best described this by referring to the research of connectivists.

We have looked at the present frameworks used to support early language and contextualised language development. In order that you can observe and record the language development of young children, we have discussed appropriate forms of observation. Young children use symbols early on in their early literacy development and we considered the role books and stories played in developing language.

Some of the challenges faced by practitioners are ways in which we can encourage early writing skills by using the environment and examples of print all around us. You will need to be aware of early input for phonics, so we have also explored this area briefly. We have looked at good practice in both of these areas to give ideas for support. We have also discussed supporting a child with learning an additional language. Finally, we have looked briefly at dyslexia and its possible challenges.

There is a vast amount written about the acquisition of language and supporting children through this vital area of development and skill. Having only visited this area in a brief way, we can conclude however that a child who is stimulated from an early age with rich interactions and warm relationships will be able to take on the immense task of learning to speak, read and write. You play an essential part in this development and need to have the correct resources and skills to motivate and encourage young children. Much of the research we have looked at has shown that listening to children is pivotal. After all, we expect them to listen to us!

CHECK YOUR UNDERSTANDING

1 What does a behaviourist perspective on language mean?

2 What is the role of nurture in children's early language development?

3 What does LAD mean?

4 What does LASS mean?

5 What do we mean by the term 'empty vessel'?

6 What do we mean by 'motherese' or 'parentese' and what is its use?

7 What did Bruce suggest is a crucial part of language development?

8 List three things you can do to support memory skills.

9 What is meant by interactionist theory?

10 What is meant by episodic memory?

11 What do we mean by procedural memory?

12 Give examples of the use of symbols.

13 Name two ways to observe language.

14 What is the difference between contextualised language and decontextualised language?

15 Give examples of how print can be used to encourage early writing skills.

16 Give at least four examples of how you can support children with phonic and graphic awareness.

17 List at least three of the challenges faced by children with dyslexia.

References and further reading

Abbott, L. and Moylett, H. (2003) *Working with the Under-Threes: Responding to children's needs*, Open University Press

Adams, M.J. (1990) *Beginning to Read: The new phonics in context*, Heinemann

Bloom, L. (1973) *Language Development: Form and function in emerging grammars*, MIT Press

Bruce, T. (2001) *Learning Through Play*, Hodder& Stoughton

Bruce, T. (2004) *Developing Learning in Early Childhood*, Paul Chapman Publications

Clay, M. (1979) *The Concepts About Print*, Heinemann

Curtis, A. and O'Hagan, M. (2003) *Care and Education in Early Childhood*, Routledge Farmer

DfES (2000) *Curriculum Guidance for the Foundation Stage*, QCA (QCA Orderline, PO Box 29, Norwich NR3 1GN, 08700 606015, ref. QCA/00/587; www.qca.org.uk/160.html)

DfES/Sure Start (2002) *Birth to Three Matters: A framework to support children in their earliest years*, DfES (DfES Publications Centre, PO Box 5050, Annesley, Nottingham NG15 0DJ, 0845 6022260; or download from www.standards.dfes.gov.uk/primary/publications/foundation_stage/9400463)

DfES (2005) Education and Skills Select Committee's enquiry into the Teaching of Reading (2005), Memorandum submitted by the DfES (Summary page of full paper); www.standards.dfes.gov.uk/primary/features/literacy/1174785/pns_nls0605evidence1.doc

Donaldson, M. (1978) *Children's Minds*, Fontana Collins

Gopnik, A., Meltzoff, A. and Kuhl, P. (2001) *How Babies Think: The science of childhood*, Phoenix

Grahame, J. and Kelly, A. (ed.) (2000) *Reading Under Control*, David Fulton

Schaffer, H.R. (2004) *Social Development*, Blackwell

Maslow, A. (1962) *Towards a Psychology of Being*, Van Nostrand

Nicholson, R.I. and Fawcett, A.J. (1990) 'Automacity: a new framework for dyslexia research', *Cognition*, vol. 30, pp 159–82

Riley, J. (2003) *Learning in the Early Years: A guide for teachers of children age 3–7*, Paul Chapman Publications

Riley, J. and Reedy, D. (2003) *Learning in the Early Years*, Paul Chapman Publications

Riddall-Leach, S. (2005) *How to Observe Children*, Heinemann

Pinker, S. (1999) *Words and Rules: The ingredients of language*, Wiedenfeld & Nicolson

Smith, P., Cowie, H. and Blades, M. (2003) *Understanding Children's Development*, Blackwell

Stern, B. (1990) *Diary of Baby*, Penguin

Vygotsky, L. (2000) *Thought and Language* (revised and edited by Alex Kozulin), MIT Press

Whitehead, M. (1999) *Supporting Language and Literacy Development*, Open University Press

Ward, S. (2004) *Baby Talk*, Arrow

Useful websites

www.dyslexiainst.org.uk – Dyslexia Institute

www.afasic.org.uk – Association for All Speech Impaired Children (AFASIC), 347 Central Markets, Smithfield, London EC1A 9NH

www.nasen.org.uk –National Association for Special Needs (NASEN)

www.earlychildhood.org.uk – Early Childhood Unit

www.standards.dfes.gov.uk – Department of Education and Skills standards site

Chapter 4

Children's relationships

Introduction

In this chapter we will look at ways in which we can understand more about how children form relationships with others. To support this understanding we will focus on relevant theories about children's relationships and link them to what we see in practice. It is vital that you are aware as a practitioner that your practice is influenced by the work of these theorists and their research findings.

As early years practitioners, we strive to understand as much as we possibly can about children – their individual needs, development, interests, behaviour and cultural backgrounds. It is vital that you have an in-depth knowledge of how children find their place in society and how they construct their earliest relationships, because with this knowledge and understanding you can support both the child and the adults around them to gain the very best from their relationships and interactions with people close to them and in the wider world.

This chapter covers:

◆ The child as a social being

◆ Constructing first relationships

◆ The beginnings and growth of intimacy and friendships

◆ The key person approach

◆ Transference.

The theorists and researchers covered in this chapter are:

◆ **Jean-Jacques Rousseau**, page 109 and 110

◆ **Sigmund Freud**, pages 109 and 136

◆ **Albert Bandura**, page 109

◆ **Lev Vygotsky**, page 110

◆ **Jerome Bruner**, page 113

◆ **Jean Piaget**, page 109

◆ **John Bowlby**, page 119

- **Mary Ainsworth**, page 124
- **Judy Dunn**, page 131
- **H. Rudolph Schaffer**, page 116
- **Elinor Goldshmeid**, **Peter Elfer** and **Dorothy Selleck**, page 134.

The child as a social being

How do children learn through social interaction?

In your practice you may sometimes wonder why some children are able to make friendships and get along with other children really well, whilst other children find relationships difficult and are often withdrawn or aggressive towards others. To consider this we might first want to look at children's social world and the part they and the adults around them play in that world.

The distinction between adults and children was not recognised until sometime in the fifteenth century. It was at this point that children started to be depicted as children. Later, in the nineteenth century, schooling became compulsory in Europe and the specific category of 'childhood' was introduced, leading to an interest in childhood as a separate time to adulthood and one worthy of further investigation. Views about childhood are still changing today and we now consider this time to be broken down into: girls and boys; babies; toddlers; school children; teenagers, with further categories being identified all the time, such as 'tweenies' (7–12-year-olds who already show teenage tendencies, for example owning mobile phones; shopping for designer clothes). Much of the research and theoretical argument has been about how children take their place in society and what factors might influence this.

THINK ABOUT IT

Think about the assumptions we make about children in our society. For example, children growing up in the 1950s had a very different childhood from children in the twenty-first century. Think about the possible differences between your own childhood and a child in the present day living in the UK in the context of:

- taking children out for a meal in a restaurant
- how children are treated in hospital
- the way in which adults consider children's viewpoints.

You might have thought about a difference in the way children are accepted and welcomed in public places and how their opinions and views are listened to more readily in the present day.

Why do you think this change has taken place?

Many leading influential theorists have looked at the relationship the child has with family, friends and the outside world. Their conclusions have formed the rationale for the ways in which we work with children today.

The table below briefly summarises some of the leading theories and theorists you need to consider when looking at the social development of children.

Theories of social development

Theory	Brief explanation
Romantic thinkers	Romantic thinkers were revolutionary in their time. They believed that children should develop naturally and not be forced into adult ways. They valued children's innocence and naturalness and felt that society could spoil this by moving them too far away from nature. The most influential of these theorists, still quoted today, is **Jean-Jacques Rousseau** – French philosopher from the 1700s.
Psychoanalytical theory	**Sigmund Freud**'s theory is well read and touches on all aspects of society. He believed that children are self-satisfying and driven by primitive impulses to have their own way (the id) and that this stage was followed by the ego, when the child tuned in to the outside world and is able to exercise restraint. He said that parents had the task of ensuring that children understand the rules of society and that from this the child's superego would emerge. Freud believed that early experience is irreversible and that childhood was a painful struggle between these three stages. More recently researchers have largely argued against his theories on child development but he did highlight the need to consider the emotional aspects of children's minds and the role of the unconscious.
Social learning theory	**Albert Bandura** emphasised learning processes and believed that children learnt through watching suitable models and imitating their behaviour. He also felt as the behaviourists did that all learning could be observed. He conducted vast amounts of empirical study, the most well-known being the Bobo doll experiment. He first felt that children would copy whatever they had seen the adult do – but he later agreed that children also had internal processes which helped them to select what they wanted to imitate.
Piagetian theory	**Piaget**'s theory was wholly concerned with cognitive functions; he paid almost no attention to social factors. His theory was a 'staged theory'. He did, however, transform thinking about the nature of development, showing us that a child is not just a miniature adult.

Freud's theories are discussed in more detail in Chapter 5, page 161.

Piaget's theories are discussed in the following chapters:

◆ *Chapter 2, How children learn, page 42*

◆ *Chapter 3, Children's communication, page 78.*

Learning through social interaction: the role of the adult

Jean-Jacques Rousseau was one of the first 'Romantic' thinkers who believed that children have a natural ability to play and therefore are closer to real freedom because they are not influenced by culture or society. He also believed that the child arrived in the world 'preformed'. By this, he meant that all aspects of their personality were already laid down. He felt, therefore, that parents had little to do with the formation of their child's personality and that they should adopt a *laissez-faire* (leave them alone and do not interfere) attitude to their upbringing so that they might achieve their full potential. **Rousseau** (cited in Schaffer, 1996), claimed that 'everything is well when it leaves the creator's hands, everything degenerates in the hands of man'.

After **Rousseau**, educationalists such as **Pestalozzi**, **A.S. Neill** and **Froebel** all adopted a similar view of children and set up schools where there was an 'unstructured' approach, giving children total freedom to explore their own interests and ideas. This was described as a *laissez-faire* model of learning.

Froebel's theories about children's play are discussed in Chapter 6, page 168, and his influence on Forest Schools in Chapter 1, page 37.

Jean-Jacques Rousseau (1712–78)

THINK ABOUT IT

Consider **Rousseau**'s viewpoint, taking note that he was writing in the eighteenth century. What are your views on the *laissez-faire* approach? You may also want to investigate the work of **Froebel** and **Pestalozzi** whose approaches were similar.

Lev Vygotsky is a well-known and respected Russian theorist . His work, which looked at the cognitive development of the child, also led him to realise that children's social transactions had an influence on their cognitive growth. He was fascinated by the fact that children are born into a world where they are surrounded by adults who are keen to help them learn. **Vygotsky** believed that the child was born with the ability to listen and remember and that it was nurturing by the adult and relationships with other people – teachers, early years practitioners and friends – that developed higher mental skills in the child. He said that social interaction, particularly with adults, supported children to develop their thinking, problem-solving and language skills. He especially noted that the zone of proximal development (ZPD) was an essential way for the adult to support the child to progress from something they know a little about to better understanding. The zone of proximal development is a sensitive time when he child will approach the adult for support and guidance. (The ZPD is also discussed in Chapter 2, page 58.)

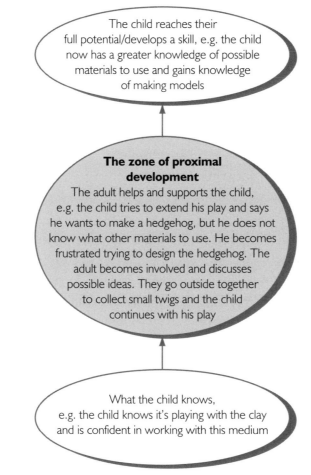

The child reaches their full potential/develops a skill, e.g. the child now has a greater knowledge of possible materials to use and gains knowledge of making models

The zone of proximal development
The adult helps and supports the child, e.g. the child tries to extend his play and says he wants to make a hedgehog, but he does not know what other materials to use. He becomes frustrated trying to design the hedgehog. The adult becomes involved and discusses possible ideas. They go outside together to collect small twigs and the child continues with his play

What the child knows, e.g. the child knows it's playing with the clay and is confident in working with this medium

Vygotsky's zone of proximal development

Vygotsky found that the ZPD could be used to encourage development of children's thinking skills through the interaction with an adult. The case study below provides an example of a time when the intervention of the practitioner could be vital.

CASE STUDY:

JAMIE AND THE FLYING MAN

Jamie is a 4-year-old child in a reception class. Recently the class have been doing lots of work about aeroplanes and similar methods of travel. Jamie has really enjoyed this topic and has worked with a group of his peers to construct a model of an aeroplane of their own design. He has also bought in pictures of space ships and flying machines collected at home with his mother. He has drawn aeroplanes in a group activity; listened to a story about the first flying machines and watched a short piece of old film showing some of the first aeroplanes.

During free play time, the early years practitioner notices that Jamie has made a clay model of a man and is trying to attach 'wing-shapes' to the model. He is becoming frustrated as he tries to make wings from a variety of materials. He models these attempts on examples he has seen in the story and on the video – lightweight materials, etc. Two of his friends are now joining in and are making suggestions to him, bringing various materials to the table to try to build wings for the clay model.

1   What would you do if you were the practitioner?

2   How would you involve yourself in this activity to support the children to reach their full potential?

3   What skills of interaction would you use to ensure that the children gained the very best from this opportunity?

Vygotsky stressed that interpersonal communication plays a vital role in the process of learning and that intervention by an adult or more knowledgeable peer will enable the child to develop as a thinker and a problem-solver.

GOOD PRACTICE CHECKLIST

Adult intervention

It is important to recognise that your role is to:

◆   build trust and openness with the children in your care so that they ask for your help or are happy for you to become involved

◆   recognise the point at which active intervention will assist the child to move on

◆   give children opportunities to ask questions; engage in debate or analyse a disagreement, for example 'Why is a man unable to fly?'

◆   make time for children to extend their ideas and work on them within the normal routine.

Good practice as described above will not only encourage freethinking but will also assist in fundamental cognitive restructuring – learning with understanding. **Vygotsky** also advocated the use of peer tutoring. This consists of an older child, who is not necessarily that far ahead of the child developmentally, working with them to support learning. He says that the impact of this communication brings out skills in both of the children. They learn to mediate and reason, internalising the learning. In the ZPD, children can, having mastered one area of understanding, help another child to put the pieces of the jigsaw together.

THINK ABOUT IT

Think about ways in which you have noticed children communicating in this way.

◆ Is peer tutoring used in your setting?

◆ If so, can you give examples of positive outcomes you witnessed or heard, for example a child understanding something they did not understand before because they have worked with a friend?

This is a way in which we can see that relationships between children can be used to support learning as well as the social understanding required for co-operation and negotiating.

Vygotsky is also discussed in the following chapters:

◆ Chapter 2, How children learn, page 58

◆ Chapter 3, Children's communication, page 78

◆ Chapter 6, Children's play, page 173.

Jerome Bruner was fascinated by the work of **Vygotsky**, particularly the role of the adult and their interactions with the child to promote development. **Bruner** and his colleagues talked about the idea of 'scaffolding' (discussed in Chapter 2, page 62). This is the role of other people in helping the child to learn and reflect on things. It cannot be achieved without relationships with other people. The adult or the 'expert peer' (an older or more experienced peer) is able to:

◆ engage the child's interest and trust – encourage the child to believe they can do it

◆ model an action – in other words 'show' the child how to do something

◆ suggest a strategy for solving a problem to support – perhaps by breaking the task into manageable parts

◆ keep the child's motivation up – encourage them to move on

◆ enable the child to climb to a higher level of understanding – through discussion; negotiating; answering questions.

This scaffolding may first appear in very early interactions, for example when the child first attempts speech. Mothers may also use scaffolding when they assist their child to express how they are feeling about something. They may encourage their child to explain how they are feeling by relating to other experiences which give them ideas to help them in expressing themselves.

CASE STUDY:

MEENA AT THE SHOPS WITH HER MOTHER

Meena is 3 years old. She is out with her mother in the shops when a large Alsatian dog comes and jumps up on her. The dog is trying to be friendly and greet the child, but Meena's response is to become upset and cry. The next morning, she is trying to recall the situation and explain how she felt to her key worker in the nursery. She says:

'The dog did jump up on me and did get … [crying] … I was crying.'

Meena's mother encourages Meena by saying, 'Was he a very big dog – was he bigger than you?' and Meena replies, 'Yes, he was as big as this.' (pointing to her sister's pushchair).

Her mother then asks, 'How did that make you feel?' and Meena replies, 'I was scared … I did cry because …' To which her mother interrupts and says, 'Because he was bigger?' Meena says, 'Yes, he was big and much bigger … I am small.'

1   What would you do to scaffold this experience for the child?

2   What might you say to the child next?

3   How would you put this experience to good use to support the child?

Bruner's theories are also discussed in the following chapters:

◆ how children learn, Chapter 2, page 62

◆ children's communication, Chapter 3, page 79

◆ supporting early literacy, Chapter 3, page 93.

The child in society

The type of society children are brought up in influences their relationships with others. Children are not, as we might imagine, only influenced by their parents, although parents are, of course, important. They are influenced by everything around them – their friends, school and community. Research carried out by **Whiting** (1986; cited in Schaffer, 2005) compared 20 communities from many parts of the world. They found that the time spent in the company of adults varied and was dependent upon such factors as economy and patterns of family life.

◆ In the Kalahari Desert in Botswana, they found that the Kung bushmen brought their children up in small family groups living a nomadic existence. Opportunities for play with other children were limited and most of their social interaction was with adults and family members – siblings and cousins.

◆ On isolated farms in northern Norway, they found that children spend all of their time with family and when they go to school, the numbers of children are very low and so education is in mixed-age groups. Older children are often responsible for much of the supervision of younger members of the community.

◆ In China and Japan, they found that group belonging and co-operation are emphasised. This is because children are more often in the company of their peers as parents are working and they may spend many hours in day care and nursery facilities.

◆ In the kibbutz system, they found that children do not live with their parents from the beginning, but live with children of their own age looked after by carers. These children are encouraged to develop skills in co-operation and dedication to collective goals rather than pursuing their own ambitions.

THINK ABOUT IT

Take time to consider and research different cultures. When you have done this, answer the following questions:

◆ Would some of these children find it difficult to make relationships in your setting?

◆ Is there provision made for children who may have different cultural backgrounds? And if so what are they?

◆ How would you enable a child from a diverse culture to make friends in your setting?

Are there cultural differences in children's friendships?

There can be no doubt that how children are brought up and the family they live in has a major influence on their social behaviour. There are many cultural varieties in child-rearing but it is not yet widely known how much these cultural influences affect the way in which children make friends. **Judy Dunn**'s (2005) research has shown that although there have been studies about friendships in many countries – China, Iceland and Germany, for example – most of the findings have shown that there is still much we do not know. It is very difficult to compare friendships in different, complex cultures because there are so many factors that could be considered. A study by **Doran French et al.** 2003 (cited in Dunn, 2005) was conducted on American and Indonesian friendships; they found there were many similarities:

◆ The children enjoyed companionship and intimacy with each other from a young age.

◆ There was similar evidence of aggression towards each other.

◆ The children displayed similar social preference and achievement in making friends.

However, there were found to be some differences in the way in which the children maintained their friendships. For example, children in Indonesia were rarely friendless and alone or rejected by their friends, whereas exclusion and withdrawal from friendships was sometimes a reality for children in America. This highlighted the need for much more research into the complexities of the culture before we can understand the detail of children's friendships.

Constructing first relationships

Early interaction and attachment

Children will form many different relationships throughout the early years with parents, grandparents, carers, siblings, peers, teachers, and so on. But it is the first relationship with their mother that has been the subject of avid research. We are given to believe that this first relationship can affect how the child relates to other people throughout their lives. To look at this very special relationship we will consider:

◆ babies – face-to-face interactions/gestures/topic sharing between the adult and the child

◆ the potential implications of missing out on early loving relationships

◆ attachment – the child's ability and need to form their first attachment

◆ the strange situation – a research method to assess security or insecurity of attachment.

H. Rudolph Schaffer (2005) is a developmental psychologist who has drawn together much of the research about children's social development. He says that the first relationships are dependent upon the adult and their co-ordination of the relationship, because the baby has very little ability to fit their behaviour to that of another person. **Schaffer** drew up the table below to show the stages in this parent–infant interaction.

Stages of parent–infant interaction

Stage	Starting age (months)	Developmental task
1 Biological regulation	0	To regulate the infant's biological processes such as feeding and waking/sleeping states and harmonise them with parental requirements
2 Face-to-face exchanges	2	To regulate mutual attention and responsiveness in face-to-face situations
3 Topic sharing	5	To incorporate objects into social interactions and ensure there is joint (adult and baby) attention and action to them

| 4 Reciprocity | 8 | To initiate intentional actions directed at others and develop more flexible and symmetrical relationships |
| 5 Symbolic representation | 18 | To develop verbal and other symbolic means of relating to others and reflect upon social exchanges |

Source: Schaffer (2005), page 110

How are you going to support this relationship between the parent and infant? You may have quite young babies in your care and need to support the mother through these stages. What does each stage mean for the mother and child? To gain a fuller understanding of how this can be supported, the table below gives some suggestions for mothers and supporting practitioners.

How the first relationships can be supported

Age	Five stages of parent–infant interaction	Ways to support parents
0 months	Biological regulation – sleep research by **Sander** et al. (1979), cited in Schaffer (2005)	Support the mother to ensure that the baby has a good routine with opportunity for good sleep patterns to be initiated. Within the first week of life, some babies will establish a sleep pattern where the longest sleep period is during the night. Whilst feeding the baby, the mother will have opportunity to bond, talk to the baby and have direct face-to-face contact.
2 months	Face-to-face exchanges	Babies experience a sharp increase in their vision – they become more aware and direct eye contact can now be made. Opportunities for this face-to-face exchange can be made at changing time as the first smiles are triggered by the eyes. The baby is now becoming aware of their mother's way of greeting them.

5 months	Topic sharing	Up to 5 months babies can be encouraged to grasp and handle objects to stimulate and amuse themselves. The baby is also able to move their attention from the mother to the toy or object. The mother can become involved and 'topic share' by following the gaze of the baby and becoming involved in their interest in that particular toy or object. The procedure the mother uses is called 'visual co-orientation'. The baby is also able to move their attention and 'study fixation' of the neonate seems to be reduced by around 3 months.
8 months	Reciprocity	The baby has many new skills. The baby can point and can follow the adult pointing. It is now that the baby can play games such as peek-a-boo and patacake. The baby will hand back a toy that the mother gives to them. The mother or carer will need to play lots of games with the baby at this stage and the child will be able to 'reciprocate'.
18 months	Symbolic representation	By 18 months and sometimes earlier, the child is now able to communicate with the mother and others. The child will use non-verbal communication in the form of gestures, for example shrugging their shoulders, as well as verbal means to communicate and make their needs known. The mother will be best placed to know what the child means. If shown an object they have not seen before, they will look at the mother or other familiar adult to seek cues from their expressions – this is called 'social referencing'.

Look at the stages described by **Schaffer** *of the baby's first interactions with the mother. Complete a series of observations on a baby interacting closely with their mother at one of the following ages: 6 weeks, 2 months, 5 months, 8 months or 18 months.*

- *Did you recognise any of the stages in parent–infant interaction? Have you seen examples of: face-to-face interactions; topic sharing; reciprocity; and social referencing?*
- *Apply the stages on the chart to your conclusion – what would your recommendations be for that baby?*

You will have found that this theory does apply to each of the developmental stages you have observed. You may have also made recommendations for the mother and child to have more opportunities to practise these skills to cement their unique relationship.

Attachment: the child's ability and need to form their first attachment

Attachment is defined as a long-term, meaningful and emotional link to a particular individual (Schaffer, 2005, page 127). Attachments have also been noted as one of the main focuses of study in developmental psychology.

The parent will have strong, innate feelings and urges to be near the child, to care for and protect them and the child will, as a result, feel secure and protected by the adult. **John Bowlby** was one of the foremost authorities on the subject of attachment.

John Bowlby (1907–90)

Bowlby was a psychiatrist who was employed by the World Health Organization to study the mental health needs of orphaned children after the Second World War. Through this work, he noted the impact separation from care-givers had on these children. In an attempt to understand the relationship between children and their key care-givers, **Bowlby** continued to study how children bond with adults and their reaction to separation from adults resulting in his attachment theory.

Bowlby found that there were four stages of attachment:

1 *Pre-attachment* – at 0–2 months the child is socially responsive to all adults.

2 *Attachment-in-the-making* – between 2 and 7 months the child begins to recognise familiar people.

3   *Clear-cut attachment* – between 7 and 24 months the child often protests at being separated from the parent, they are wary of strangers and will let others know this is how they feel.

4   *Goal-corrected partnership* – from 24 months onwards children begin to understand parents' needs and their relationships become more two-sided.

This mother is giving comfort – the beginnings of a secure base for the child

The child will form this attachment to the parent in the majority of situations. **Bowlby** also found in his research that children first begin to miss their parents at around 7 or 8 months. At this time, a fear of strangers also emerges and unknown strangers are greeted with wariness or avoided. **Bowlby** called this 'separation anxiety' or 'separation distress'. He also told us that children have an in-built bias at first to form an attachment to one person, normally the mother, which he referred to as 'monotropism'. He told us that a baby by nature is only capable of forming one of these unique and special relationships. But this has since proven to be wrong by further and more recent research. **Schaffer and Emerson** (1964a; cited in Schaffer, 2005) studied 60 infants in their first 18 months of life and found that almost one-third of the babies studied formed attachments to more than one person and that by 18 months the majority were attached to more than one individual.

CASE STUDY:

THE EFE PYGMIES

The Efe pygmies are a semi-nomadic people in Zaire, Central Africa. During the first year of their lives the children of this tribe have many caretakers whilst their mothers work. Other women might pick the baby up and comfort it by putting it to the breast whether they are lactating or not. The babies are nearly always held in close contact. The children in this tribe were found to be secure and happy and held a strong group identity, which is useful in their particular environment.

Source: Tronick and Morelli (1992), cited in Schaffer (2005), page 136

1 Why would a strong group identity be useful in such an environment?

2 What would be the disadvantages of a child having many care-givers in our society?

3 What are the advantages of being held in close contact for a young baby?

4 Could you envisage this kind of early child-rearing practices working with the children in your care?

Key features of Bowlby's attachment theory

◆ Children show a marked preference for closeness to a small number of adults and these attachments are a normal and universal part of child development.

◆ Babies need to form attachments not primarily for food but for the comfort and security that attachments bring.

◆ Individuals other than the mother can be selected to form attachments. Nor does the main attachment figure have to be a woman.

◆ A mother can be apart from her child for several hours a day and yet still have the same relationship with the child and offer comfort and security.

◆ Adults who offer a sensitive response to the child are often missed by the child when they are absent.

◆ Attachment behaviour, the baby's actions which bring about physical contact with their attachment figure, increases when the baby feels frightened, and decreases when the baby feels safe and secure.

◆ As babies grow and mature, the need for attachment figures becomes less. However, attachment behaviour continues as we return for comfort and reassurance in times of stress or anxiety.

◆ Our own individual experience of attachment in infancy influences our closest relationships throughout life.

THINK ABOUT IT

Consider the way in which children of different ages respond to leaving their parent or carer. What strategies and preparation would you put in place if a child of 14 months were starting in your setting?

In your practice, however, you will have had different experiences of children's responses to early separation and leaving their main carer for the first time. This can be very distressing for both the child and the adult. The theories on attachment and bonding can be used to underpin your practice. It is essential that every situation is seen on its own merit and every child is seen as an individual as this may be the first time they have experienced separation and it requires a sympathetic approach.

You might have considered strategies such as the ones in the checklist below.

GOOD PRACTICE CHECKLIST

Supporting a child starting in a setting

◆ Carry out a home visit. The key worker visits the child and parent at home to get to know the child in familiar surroundings and build a trust between with the child and the parent.

◆ Questionnaires filled out by the parent will tell you about things such as the child's favourite toy, the way they like to be put down for a sleep, how frequently the child likes a drink, favourite toys or comforter, sleep patterns, food likes and dislikes, favourite nursery rhyme, how they like to be held and comforted, etc.

◆ Allow the child to bring familiar things to the setting when they start, for example sheets or blankets; cups or bottles.

◆ Invite the parent and child to visit the setting before the child begins as a prelude to the settling-in period when the parent is able to stay with the child.

◆ Encourage the child to get to know the setting, by giving them the opportunity to explore it whilst the parent is still there.

◆ Make a gradual introduction to the setting to settle the child in.

◆ Explain to the child, read stories and ask the parent to read the same story.

◆ Keep familiar things for the child in their special place – a bag or a box with a picture the child has chosen or a photo of the child on it.

There is more about **Bowlby**'s attachment theory in Chapter 5, How children feel, page 159.

TRY IT OUT

Having thought about ways in which you will help the child to settle, formulate a questionnaire to give to parents which asks questions about the child. You will be asking the parents to share information about the child which only they might know so this would need to be written sensitively. Produce it in a format that you would be happy to give to the parent – don't forget to make sure it is marked 'Confidential' and that you ensure this for the parent only.

Proximity and security or insecurity of attachment

In looking at how children construct their first relationships, **Schaffer** says that there is a behaviour that is part of attachment and that this is the way in which very young children express those feelings. A baby is completely helpless as a newborn and therefore needs the parent to be very close and protect them.

Schaffer characterised attachments the following ways:

- ◆ *Selective* – the baby will focus on individuals, usually the parents, and this selectiveness is not found in relationships with other people.

- ◆ *Physical proximity seeking* – the baby wants and needs to be physically close to the person with whom they form their main attachment. This is seen in all of the higher animal species.

- ◆ *Comfort and security* – when the baby has achieved proximity, comfort and security are the result.

- ◆ *Separation distress* – when the baby is separated from the mother (or main attachment) and they cannot achieve proximity.

Schaffer also clarifies that focused attachments become evident between 7 and 8 months, although the ability to recognise familiar people is much earlier. Between 6 and 12 months babies become capable of person permanence, remaining 'orientated to individuals' even in their absence (Schaffer, 2005, page 153).

CASE STUDY:
LAURA

Laura is 2 months old. She is has just woken from a sleep and her mother's friend is holding her. The friend talks to her and holds her in her arms, stroking her face whilst her mother is busy doing something else. Laura is content with this for some time but soon becomes fractious and starts to cry. The friend walks around with her and sings to her trying to comfort her but Laura cannot be comforted. When she is handed back to her mother, Laura immediately becomes calmer, and her cries quieten when her mother begins to sing to her and hold her against her shoulder with her head supported. Laura's mother tells her friend, 'She really likes it when you hold her like this and this is her favourite song.'

1 Why do you think Laura may have found more comfort in the way her mother handled her?

2 Would it be possible for the friend to emulate this relationship given more time?

3 Do you think Laura recognised her mother in other ways? If so, how?

4 Do you think Laura had formed an attachment to her mother?

The strange situation experiment

In 1978 **Mary Ainsworth** and her colleagues devised an experiment or procedure to assess security of attachment in young babies (see below). From these experiments, **Ainsworth** discovered more about how social relationships are first established and stated that the way in which a child forms this earliest attachment will influence their future relationships. There has been much debate about her theory and many believe that temperament of the child and the adults involved are also influential. **Ainsworth** carried out tests on children and their mothers to further explore the ways in which children react to adults.

The 'strange situation' test is carried out in the following way:

The strange situation experiment

The following seven steps are carried out in an unfamiliar room watched by observers through a two-way mirror. Each step lasts about 3 minutes. The main aim of the experiment is to see how the baby will react each time and how much the baby will make use of the mother as a source of comfort after each separation.

Step 1: The baby plays while the mother watches.

Step 2: A stranger enters the room. First they are silent and then they talk to the mother. Next they begin to play with the baby.

Step 3: The mother leaves the room and the stranger continues to play with the baby.

Step 4: The mother then returns to the room and comforts the baby if need be. The stranger leaves the room.

Step 5: The mother leaves the room again leaving the baby alone.

Step 6: The stranger comes into the room again and plays with the baby.

Step 7: The mother returns for the last time and, depending upon the baby's reaction, will comfort the baby or continue as normal; the stranger leaves the room.

THINK ABOUT IT

Consider the babies you know.

◆ How do you think they would react to this type of experiment?

◆ Do you think they would become upset, and if so for how long?

◆ What do you feel would be the cause, or causes, of their upset?

◆ What would you think about a baby who did not become distressed or concerned about the absence of their mother and the arrival of a stranger in the room?

If you have ever watched a recording of one of these experiments you may have found it a little upsetting, as very often the babies become very distressed. In answering the questions above, you may have thought that many of the babies you have known would not have become distressed had it not been for the strange environment and unknown situation.

Ainsworth said that the reactions of the babies to this experiment could be classified into three attachment types (shown in the table below); type D (insecure/disorganised) was added later, but it is usually the first three which are more commonly referred to.

Three types of attachment

Type	The behaviour of the baby in the 'strange situation'
Type A – insecurely attached – avoidant	The baby appears to avoid contact with the mother especially when she leaves the room or comes back into the room. When the baby is left with a stranger the baby does not appear to be particularly distressed.
Type B – securely attached	The baby appears to want to be near the mother but is not necessarily seeking her attention. The baby is upset when the mother leaves but is happy to see her when she comes back.
Type C – insecurely attached – resistant	The baby is very distressed when separated from the mother. When the mother returns she finds it difficult to console the baby, the baby wants comfort from the mother but also rejects being comforted at the same time.

Babies who fall into type B (about 65 per cent of the babies in the majority of studies carried out in the USA) were considered by **Ainsworth** to be more likely to form positive relationships throughout life. There have been some criticisms of this theory of attachment:

◆ There can be more than these classifications of attachment – more ways in which babies can be attached to a parent.

◆ Cultural variations – children from other cultures and societies often demonstrated a tendency towards other types of attachment. This could be dependent upon particular child-rearing practices and also the influence of the setting which would seem more stressful to some babies than to others (Van Ijzendoorn and Kroonenberg, 1998; cited in Schaffer, 2005).

◆ The experiment was carried out on very young babies and further studies with older children were difficult to assess and measure in the same way.

◆ There are many factors which might affect attachment which can change throughout the early years of life – outside events, for example, which could change the ability of the mother to be sensitive to the baby's needs.

Sensitivity

Ainsworth said that babies form secure relationships with their mother in these first few months of life because the mother is sensitive in her response to the baby. If the mother should fail to respond in this way, it will result in the baby being insecurely attached. The case studies below show the particular ways in which mothers respond to their babies in each of the three attachment types.

CASE STUDY:

TYPE A – INSECURE/AVOIDANT

Charlotte is 5 months old and her mother feels she is doing an adequate job of looking after her. She is often tired and is a little depressed at times, but she always ensures that Charlotte is fed and changed. She likes to get on with chores while Charlotte is quiet and doesn't really have time to play with her. She finds Charlotte hard work to interact with as she doesn't really know what to do with her. She would rather have had a boy.

CASE STUDY:

TYPE B – SECURE

Mukund is 8 months old and his mother enjoys being with him. She is quickly able to pick up signals from him if he needs her. For example, she recognises certain types of crying as 'being hungry' or 'needs a cuddle'. When Mukund is very wakeful one night, his mother is accepting of this change in his normal routine even though she is tired! When he is awake, she plays face-to-face with him as much as possible and encourages smiles and communication.

CASE STUDY:

TYPE C – INSECURE/RESISTANT

George is 6 months old and his mother is unhappy since having her baby, but feels guilty that she should be a better mother. She has good days and bad days with George and sometimes has broken sleep making it hard the following day to cope. George's mother loves to give him a cuddle sometimes because he has been so good, but sometimes she really can't be bothered with him as he has been so difficult the night before. When George cries, she is never sure what it is he needs.

You may have considered the other possible factors in the lives of these families and the possible resulting impact on the child when looking at these case studies. The mothers may have been responding in this way because of external factors such as economic or environmental challenges or they may be suffering from post-natal depression. There have been criticisms of this theory as it is has been felt that further research needed to be carried out to consider the views of the parents involved and that there has not been enough proof to link these early relationships to other social competencies later in the child's life.

In 1994, research carried out by **Elinor Goldschmeid** and her colleagues showed that between birth and 3 years old all children need:

◆ responsive loving attention
◆ opportunities to develop positive self-identity
◆ opportunities to develop interdependent relationships
◆ unconditional acceptance from the people in their lives.

Source: Goldschmeid et al. (2003)

Although parents cannot respond to every cue from their child, it is clear that those parents who are emotionally sensitive to their children's needs provide security for their child which enables the child to become more socially competent in their lives.

Much of the recent research shows that attachments can change over time and that mothers can change their attitudes to children as they grow older, preferring different phases of development. Babies can form more than one attachment as they are born to be social beings and they will not suffer as a result of having more than one person in their life to care for them. **Werner** (1996, cited in Maynard and Thomas, 2004) studied a group of high-risk children through to adulthood and said that, 'the most important ingredient is a significant person in the child's life to whom the child and what they do "matters".'

THINK ABOUT IT

◆ What can you do to promote these early relationships?
◆ How can you make use of the secure relationship with the parents to ensure that the child feels secure in the setting?

You may have considered some of the following ideas for good practice.

GOOD PRACTICE CHECKLIST

Interacting with young babies

◆ Ensure that respect is given to the parent or main carer as the child's *first educator and carer.*
◆ Ask the parent or main carer for their advice in dealing with the handling of very young children, for example how to get the baby to sleep, comforters, favourite songs and nursery rhymes.
◆ Be sensitive to the child's needs and take cues from the parent in what these might be.
◆ Encourage secure attachments with the child – face-to-face interaction, smiles and communication.
◆ Be understanding and supportive to the child and the parent/carer during the initial separation period.

The beginnings of friendship and the growth of intimacy

We have looked at how children begin their lives by constructing their first relationships, usually with their parents. We have considered that these first relationships are essential in preparing the child for future relationships with other people. We also looked at ways in which you can support parents in these early interactions and how the child is able to have many of these early close experiences with the adults in their lives. We will next consider how children begin to make their own relationships through choice, the beginnings of this early intimacy with another person and the resulting friendships.

Young children begin to develop a sense of self from a very young age. Children who may have experienced maltreatment from their parents may see themselves as unloved or unworthy. To have empathy for others and to begin to care about others is a part of development that can be affected by the way young children have been cared for. What we next need to ask is: 'When do children begin to see themselves as separate from others and begin to appreciate the other person's point of view?' In 1980, **R. Selman** created a table of stages of development in children's understanding of self and others. The table below describes the stages and gives examples of how we might see this in the practical sense:

Stages in a child's understanding of self and others

Stage and age	Type of understanding	Practical examples
Stage 0 3–6 years	At the beginning of this stage the child is egocentric – everything centres around them and they have no understanding of how others may see a situation differently. There is a shift at around 14–16 months and children will begin to form views on what they 'like' and 'dislike'.	Two-year-old Tom is playing in the sandpit alongside Jason. Tom is throwing the sand around and has upset Jason who wants to sit in the middle of the sandpit as part of his imaginary game. When the adult explains that Jason's game is just as important to him as Tom's game is to him, Tom appears unable to understand how Jason is feeling.

Stage 1 5–9 years	The child begins to recognise that there are different viewpoints but cannot always relate these viewpoints to each other.	Rina is sitting with an adult looking through a picture book. David comes over and asks if he can have a story read as well. Rina is upset and says that she was promised a story on her own. The adult explains that David has been very unhappy today and that sharing this time would make him feel happy. Rina says, 'OK then. I suppose it's OK.' Later Rina has to be asked to understand David's situation again when he wants to share the computer with her. This time she does not share and leaves the computer.
Stage 2 7–12 years	The child can now reflect on another person's viewpoint, but cannot consider both the other person's view and their own at the same time.	Two children are arguing over who has the red shepherd's costume for the school play. The adult explains to George that Ben was not able to wear this costume last year because he was unwell. George wants to be sympathetic but finds it difficult, as he really wants to wear the costume!
Stage 3 10–15 years	Different viewpoints can now be reviewed simultaneously. The child can now see how the other person may feel about their viewpoint.	Kelly and Sarah are having a discussion in class about who should be the basketball captain. They have opposing views but are able to discuss their viewpoints without falling out and come to an amicable conclusion.
Stage 4 15 years–adult	People can now make comparisons of points of view and generalise about the views of society in an abstract way.	Young people and adults have a growing and developing awareness of different points of view and can compare different viewpoints. For example, Katy and Sophie (both teenagers) have a discussion about their political views. They are open to listening to each other's viewpoint and also call on other advantages and disadvantages in the discussion.

THINK ABOUT IT

Think of examples of this understanding of others in your setting. You may want to consider possible ways the adult can be involved in this process. For example, how can the adult help support a child in one of the earlier stages to interpret another child's perspective without using coercion tactics?

Children develop skills throughout the early years to support them in relationships with the people around them. As we have already said, this begins with their first relationships and their family/home environment. The child is also reliant upon a 'sense of belonging'. The New Zealand Ministry of Education (1996, page 54) states that all children need to have a sense of belonging because 'it contributes to their inner well-being, security and identity'. This sense of belonging is not only important in the family but also in nursery and school. Young children need to feel wanted and valued by the people they spend time with – peers, practitioners, other adults. Early years settings need to promote and advocate a sense of belonging and give children opportunities to interact with each other and make friends.

What constitutes a friendship?

There has been a great deal of debate amongst researchers as to what constitutes a friendship. We know as early years practitioners that it is important that children learn to get on with each other and it is opportune when children become friends!

CASE STUDY:

KIRSTY AND EMILY

Kirsty and Emily started nursery together and before that attended pre-school together. At nursery they are always together and spend much of their time in elaborate fantasy play. Occasionally they are princesses in a castle running from the dragon and hiding together under the table. More often than not they play together in the theme corner in the post office or teashop, playing out a variety of adult roles. They have been known to be completely exclusive in their adventures, telling other children to 'please leave and come back later' or 'maybe you can play tomorrow'. They are completely engrossed in their play and each one appears to know and understand what the other means. They solve problems together and initiate new games and scenarios – 'I know – you can be the baby and let me take you to the park.'

1 Would you describe Emily and Kirsty's relationship as a friendship?

2 What sorts of skills do you think they are learning from each other?

3 What do you think they have in common with each other?

You may have thought that the girls' relationship could be described as a friendship and would certainly be seen as a friendship by their parents. It would seem evident that the girls are co-operating and learning new skills from each other. The girls do have much in common in terms of familiarity and they share an interest in the same fantasy play.

CASE STUDY:

RELATIONSHIPS WITH OBJECTS

Laura is 2 years 8 months. She has had a small soft pink bear since she was born and she calls him Pinky Bear.

Laura is playing in her bedroom. Around her are many of her toys – she is sitting on the floor with her legs straight out in front of her and Pinky Bear is under her arm. While she pretends to pour into a cup she is speaking to Pinky Bear, 'Here you are –it is juice for you Pinky Bear.' She holds Pinky Bear up on her lap and puts the cup to his mouth, 'Do you like it? Do you?' she whispers.

Later the adult is sitting with Laura. She has a small finger puppet on her finger and is talking to Laura through the puppet, 'Will you give me some juice Laura – like you give Pinky Bear?' Laura looks very seriously at the finger puppet , 'No'. The puppet (adult) asks her, 'Why not Laura?' She replies very gently, 'Because you haven't got a mouth.'

1   Would you say that Laura has a relationship with Pinky Bear?

2   How would you describe the relationship?

3   Is there a difference between Laura's relationship with the bear and the puppet?

You may have suggested that Laura sees the bear as a comforter. Children communicate in an imaginative way with objects and can have short periods of time when they appear to trust the object almost as much as a human being.

THINK ABOUT IT

You might want to investigate these particular relationships in more detail – or take note of the ways in which young children communicate with loved objects. When does this stop happening?

Judy Dunn (2005) has researched and written about the importance of understanding children's friendships and explains that observing children with their friends can provide us with a window 'on what children know and understand about the social world' (page 5). Her research looks at the feelings friendships elicit in children – jealousy, loyalty, caring and empathy. This research also revealed the differences between friendships and sibling relationships. For example, children are often more patient with their friends trying to resolve differences and will respond to their needs and feelings; whereas in their relationships with siblings they do not always appear to be very worried about resolutions and even appear to enjoy the power struggle disagreements create. It has been shown that friendships are closely linked to children's sense of moral understanding. Because children care about their friends, they will consider their needs and rights and display loyalty in defending them. This point was also made by **Piaget** (cited in Dunn (2005), page 7) who said, 'arguments between children are of special significance in the growth of children's understanding of moral issues.'

Dunn showed that the early relationships between children told us much about children:

◆ The process of early friendships even in very young children are unique and demonstrate a child's ability to care about another child.

◆ These first relationships are very different from those with parents, siblings and other family members.

◆ Friends can have an influence on the child's actions. This can be in a positive and a negative way.

◆ Children can have intense feelings about their friends and this, in addition to the familiarity and intimacy of the relationship, can have a profound influence on the child's social development and self-confidence.

◆ We can see the impact of early friendships on how the child will learn to deal with supporting others, sharing secrets and communicating.

◆ The formation of these relationships underpins the beginning of children's moral understanding.

Very young children can form friendships based on shared pretend

THINK ABOUT IT

Try to remember your first friend. When you do this, consider all the feelings linked with that early friendship. What sort of emotions do you think of?

You may have thought of many different emotions – loyalty, jealousy, closeness and even rejection. **Dunn** considered that even very young children can have real friendships and that these are very common in the nursery age. She says that children very definitely 'choose' the person with whom they will play, with mutual interests and ideas being one of the major reasons for their choice. Although very young children lack the ability to understand others' feelings or have empathy, they will become involved in a world of 'shared pretend' with another child. The children will share an imaginary world and take part in make-believe play. This can help them develop skills in communication, supportive behaviour, trust and mutual understanding.

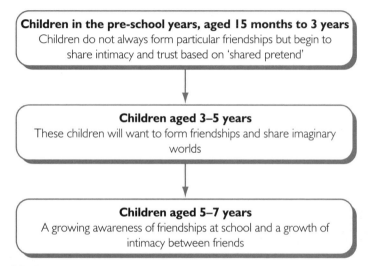

Children in the pre-school years, aged 15 months to 3 years
Children do not always form particular friendships but begin to share intimacy and trust based on 'shared pretend'

Children aged 3–5 years
These children will want to form friendships and share imaginary worlds

Children aged 5–7 years
A growing awareness of friendships at school and a growth of intimacy between friends

The progress of friendship awareness

THINK ABOUT IT

You might want to look in more detail at friendships between children and research:

◆ friendships in a social world

◆ the advantages of friendships during transition

◆ girls and boys and friendship.

You can find more information from the studies of **Dunn** and her colleagues (2005).

Looking at relationships in the setting

One of the best ways to look at the way in which children in your care are making relationships is through the use of observation and sociograms. These can help you to gain a greater understanding of children's relationships with each other. The information can also help you to support children who may be having difficulties and perhaps make changes to the environment to facilitate better access for some children.

You can use:

- time sampling charts, noting down at different times of the day who is playing with whom – ideal for large groups of children
- flow charts (see the example below) to track a child's, or group of children's, movements around the room showing where they become involved with activities and other children.

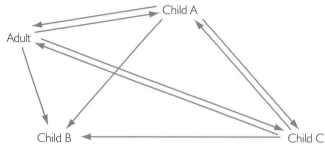

Source: Riddal-Leech (2005), page 40

An example of a flow chart sociogram

In the flow chart above, it is easy to see where one child has moved throughout the session, but you can also do these for small groups of children.

> ### TRY IT OUT
>
> *Try observing in your setting using one of these forms of sociogram. You may want to look at one child (perhaps a child who is isolated from the group) or a small group of children (this might be a group of girls, for example, who always play together).*
>
> *When you have done this, consider the following questions:*
> - *What has this told you about the movements of the particular child or group?*
> - *Have you noticed anything you did not see before?*
> - *What changes will you consider making as a result of this observation?*

The key person approach

The children in your care will form friendships and relationships with other children and this is key to their social development. When children leave the security of their families, they also need to make new relationships with adults who will support the family to care for and educate them in the early years. This relationship is also a special one as it may be the first trusting relationship made outside the family. If a child is to be looked after by a home-based carer, this can be easier as there is still a one-to-one intimacy involved. However, in nurseries this can be a little more difficult to achieve. **Goldschmeid, Elfer and Selleck** (2003) advocate the key person approach. The key person can ensure that the child feels special and unique and is worthy of one person's special attention. The key person can provide:

- the child with a sense of security and continuity
- a 'special' relationship with the child
- understanding and knowledge of the child
- individual planning with the family
- support for the mother or main carer and give them peace of mind
- a close physical presence to the child during the settling-in period
- close relationship with the family to sustain connections with home.

Goldschmeid *et al.* state that this role is vital in nursery provision and that nurseries should make a commitment to this approach. They also give advice on ways in which the approach can be implemented:

- research the setting and reflect on the relevance of a key person approach
- give staff the opportunity to develop the idea
- make a statement of commitment to the approach
- discuss the practical realities.

THINK ABOUT IT

- What are the advantages and disadvantages of a key person approach?
- What strategies could be put into place in an early years setting to facilitate such an approach?

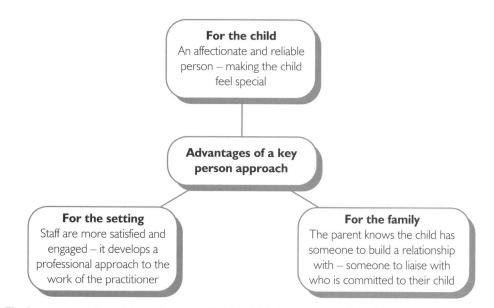

The key person approach has advantages for the child, the nursery and the family

The key person approach

◆ The key person should have regular supervision to support them in their role.

◆ Additional time will be needed for training and planning for key persons.

◆ Rotas, holiday schedules and training programmes must take account of the key person's time being managed.

◆ The setting should have a key-person policy for settling children in and their relationships with the families.

◆ The adult:child ratio should relate to the time needed for working with children and their families.

◆ Children's intimate care should be mostly carried out by the key person.

◆ Children should have the opportunity to spend time with their key person's group.

◆ Where possible, children should have the opportunity to communicate in their home language.

◆ The key person should obtain and keep the records of their key child in line with the confidentiality policy of setting.

Transference

The practitioner is important in providing the stability and continuity in these first trusting relationships with the child. These relationships, however, can be vulnerable to stirring feelings within the practitioner. **Sigmund Freud** identified transference when he noticed that his patients often seemed to fall in love with him – including the men. Fortunately, he realised that this was caused by something other than his magnetic personality. Transference occurs when a person takes the perceptions and expectations of one person and projects them onto another person, as illustrated in the following case study.

CASE STUDY: CHARLOTTE

Charlotte was training to be an early years practitioner. She felt she was doing particularly well in her practical placement at the nursery. She was so attached to the children, especially one child, Annie, who followed her around all day. Annie was very shy and Charlotte had been drawn to her immediately. Charlotte knew that Annie loved her to give her special attention. She did not always ask Annie to perform the same tasks as the other children because she felt that Annie was shy and should not be made to do everything. The nursery supervisor asked to speak to Charlotte's tutor – she had concerns that Charlotte was making a favourite of Annie and not allowing her to be involved in activities. When the tutor and the supervisor approached Charlotte about this, she said she felt she understood Annie as she had also been very shy in school and did not want to be involved in everything as she did not have the confidence to join in.

1 What are your first thoughts on Charlotte's view of Annie?

2 What effects do you think Charlotte may or may not be having on Annie's development?

3 What advice do you think the tutor and the supervisor should give to Charlotte?

You may have found this case study interesting. As an objective observer, you will have seen that there was transference taking place and that Charlotte was unaware of this and felt she was acting in Annie's best interest. It is important that you are aware of your own insecurities and emotional challenges, and this often comes with the ability to be a reflective practitioner, and making a commitment to leaving our own needs and challenges at home to become an empathic practitioner.

Summary

In this chapter we have considered the social world and development of children, firstly looking at their place in society and considering some of the expectations of family and culture. We have discussed some of the key theorists in social development to consider the various ways children's social development has been researched and analysed. Some of the researchers we have considered here have examined the influences on a child's development from the parent and the immediate environment. Are children open vessels to be filled up with knowledge or are they born with an innate ability to communicate and form relationships?

We have also looked at how children construct their first relationships and form bonds and attachments with their mothers. These bonds and attachments are said to have an affect on how children form relationships later in their lives. We have looked briefly at early friendships and the shared worlds of imaginary and pretend play. In early years settings, the adults also become closely involved with young children to provide the right balance of care and education that supports their relationships with others. In order that you can offer a sound and secure environment with adequate stimulation, systems will need to be put in place to ensure the child is offered good continuity of care. Although not possible or indeed practical in all early years environments, we considered the advantages of a key person approach and the ways in which this might be implemented. We then briefly discussed the complex issue of transference and examined the possible effects on practice, to raise an awareness for you of the need to understand where your upbringing and life experiences might have influenced your perceptions of relationships with children.

As we said at the beginning of this chapter, it is vital that you have an in-depth knowledge of how children find their place in society and how they construct their earliest relationships. It is important to know this because with this knowledge and understanding we can support both the child and the adults around them to gain the very best from their relationships and interactions with people close to them and in the wider world.

CHECK YOUR UNDERSTANDING

1 What is the *laissez-faire* model of learning?

2 Give an example of ZPD.

3 Give an example of scaffolding.

4 What sort of involvement would children have with their families in China?

5 How is the 'strange situation' experiment carried out?

6 What is topic sharing?

7 What is meant by reciprocity?

8 Name Bowlby's four stages of development.

9 Clarify what physical proximity seeking means.

10 What is the definition of a secure attachment?

11 What do we mean by a sense of belonging?

12 What do we mean by shared pretend?

13 Give examples of ways to conduct a sociogram.

14 What is meant by transference?

References and further reading

Abbott, L. and Moylett, H. (2005) *Working with the Under-Threes: Responding to children's needs*, Open University Press

Ainsworth, M.D.S (1991) *Patterns of Attachment*, Lawrence Erlbaum Associates

Dunn, J. (1993) *Young Children's Close Relationships Beyond Attachment*, Sage

Dunn, J. (2005) *Children's Friendships: The beginning of intimacy*, Blackwell

Goldschmeid, E., Elfer, P. and Selleck, D. (2003) *Key Persons in the Nursery*, David Fulton

Riddall-Leech, S. (2005) *How to Observe Children*, Heinemann

Smith, P.K., Cowie, H. and Blades, M. (2004) *Understanding Children's Development*, Blackwell

Maynard, T. and Thomas, N. (2004) *An Introduction to Early Childhood Studies*, Sage

Schaffer, H.R. (2005) *Social Development*, Blackwell

Chapter 5

How children feel

Introduction

From birth, children rapidly develop their ability to experience and express different emotions as well as their capacity to cope with and manage a variety of feelings. Most of these abilities are in place by the time children are 2 years old. The development of these abilities occurs at the same time as a wide range of more visible skills: physical, intellectual and communication. In the past, emotional development has received relatively less recognition than these other core areas of development. As an early years practitioner, it is important for you to recognise the foundation that emotional development establishes for later growth and development. It is essential for young children's feelings to receive the same level of recognition and attention as other areas of their development.

Self-awareness, life skills (going to the bathroom by themselves, dressing themselves and taking care of their own belongings), conflict management and self-esteem are all extremely important aspects of being social. Emotions affect our social behaviour and many of the choices we make are also influenced by emotions. Learning to manage feelings and emotions can be very difficult for some children and can result in later psychological difficulties if not appropriately supported early on by adults around them. It is with alarming regularity that we hear about how adults with emotional problems can trace them back to some difficulty in childhood (Dowling, 2000). **Goleman** (1998) says that early childhood is a critical time for supporting and nurturing emotional growth; if opportunities are missed it becomes harder to compensate for this at a later date. If you are going to prevent these difficulties for the children in your care in later life, and support emotional well-being in general, you need to take advantage of the receptive nature of young children and support the development of their emotional health.

The key features of emotional development which occur during early childhood are given in the table below.

The key features of emotional development

Feature	Explanation
The ability to identify and understand one's own feelings	The self-awareness of recognising a feeling as it happens to you, being honest with yourself about how you feel
Motivating yourself	Dealing with emotions to be able to concentrate and focus your feelings in a productive way which in turn impacts on learning
To manage strong emotions and express them appropriately	Handling feelings so that they are appropriate for the situation – an ability that builds upon self-awareness
To develop empathy for others	The ability to empathise, including being able to notice social signals and tune into the emotions of other people
To establish and sustain relationships	Social relationships depend on using empathy to support other people and help manage the emotional content of relationships

The success of young children's emotional development is very dependent on their individual personal experiences, the quality of social interactions with others and the influences of the environments in which they live. Emotional development and social development are very closely linked, with one affecting the other. Emotional development is also greatly influenced by young children's perceptions of how accepted they feel by those around them, including their peers as well as teachers. Through their work, **Freud**, **Rogers** and **Bowlby** have all drawn conclusions about how young children develop emotionally. Their thinking has greatly influenced practice today.

This chapter covers:

◆ Emotional intelligence

◆ Sense of self

◆ Self-esteem

◆ Coping with feelings

◆ How adults interact with children

◆ Key theories about how children feel.

The theorists and researchers covered in this chapter are:

◆ **Abraham Maslow**, page 144

◆ **Erik Erikson**, page 153

◆ **John Bowlby**, page 159

◆ **Sigmund Freud**, page 161

◆ **Carl Rogers**, page 162.

Emotional intelligence

It is important to recognise and value the emotional development of young children. Feelings, self-awareness, life skills, conflict management and self-esteem are all critically important throughout life. **Macintyre** (2002) recognises that healthy emotional development enables children to:

- approach new situations with confidence
- express feelings and emotions
- cope with anxieties and to be more resilient
- enjoy problem-solving
- appreciate works of art, music and dance
- cry if they want to
- understand the perception of other people
- appreciate the atmosphere, for example in a church
- be innovative and imaginative.

Howard Gardner (1983) recognised that emotions and intelligence were closely linked, believing that there are several types of independent intelligences, including:

- intrapersonal intelligence – the ability to understand, identify and control one's own feelings
- interpersonal intelligence – the ability to understand, label and influence the emotions of others.

Although these different kinds of intelligence usually go together, having one kind does not guarantee that you'll have the other. From **Gardner**'s work, **Goleman** developed the concept of 'emotional intelligence'. He defines emotional intelligence as knowing one's own feelings and using them to make good decisions in life. Emotional intelligence is the capacity to acquire and apply information of an emotional nature, to feel and respond emotionally (Goleman, 1998). Emotional intelligence enables people to be able to understand what others are feeling, managing emotions in relation to others and being able to persuade and lead others (Pound, 2005). In the last decade, research has discovered a tremendous amount about the role emotions play in our lives. It is believed that, even more than IQ, emotional awareness and the ability to handle feelings will determine your success in later life and in forming relationships.

Emotionally intelligent people often share the following skills and attributes:

- self-awareness
- empathy
- impulse control
- listening skills
- decision-making skills
- anger management skills.

Research in brain development has identified a clear link between emotions and learning. Children who are exposed to both long- and short-term stressful situations are taken over by a survival instinct and their ability to learn productively is greatly reduced. As an early years practitioner, you will know that children who are upset or distressed are unable to actively take part in learning, and you will be aware that there are times when children's emotional needs must be addressed before they can be receptive to learning. **Abraham Maslow**'s (1962) theory, the hierarchy of needs, illustrates this by demonstrating that there are levels of needs that must be met before learning (self-actualisation) can take place (see the diagram below). **Maslow** believed that it is only when all of these needs are met that we are able to fulfil our potential.

Maslow's hierarchy of needs

We therefore need to ensure that the learning environment is emotionally positive and supportive. We need to provide environments that recognise children's feelings and that encourage children to feel, think and talk about their feelings.

We can provide an environment that is emotionally supportive by ensuring that it:

- is physically safe and secure
- is stimulating
- meets the needs of all of the children
- supports decision-making and problem-solving
- enables children to make choices
- promotes positive relationships between staff, parents, children and the community
- recognises feelings and deals with them appropriately
- promotes self-esteem
- encourages and celebrates success
- respects and values each and every child
- has flexible but regular routines.

Write a description of how your setting ensures that each of the above points are met.
Ask a colleague from another setting to carry out the same task, and share and compare your ideas.
Are there any changes that could be made to improve the quality of emotional support?

To meet the needs of the children and foster an environment that positively supports emotional development, it is vital that you have a sound understanding of the social and emotional developmental transitions (see the table below). These are often difficult to pinpoint, as they are less obvious than physical milestones. However, they are equally, if not more, important.

Social and emotional developmental transitions

Age	Transition
Birth–3 months	Babies eagerly explore the environment around them, including themselves and other people. Infants are usually very social and are interested in other people and quickly learn to recognise their primary carers. Most babies: ◆ can be comforted by a familiar adult ◆ respond positively to touch ◆ smile and show pleasure in response to social stimulation.
3–6 months	Babies continue to enjoy increasing amounts of social interaction. They can: ◆ smile ◆ laugh aloud ◆ recognise own name ◆ are more visually responsive to language than earlier in their development ◆ enjoy repetitive games, songs and rhymes.
6–9 months	Babies begin to show a clearer range of emotional responses. They begin to show a preference for a principal carer. They can: ◆ express a wider range of emotions ◆ distinguish family members from strangers ◆ respond positively to language ◆ show displeasure at the loss of a toy.
9–12 months	Babies are developing their independence. They can: ◆ begin to feed themselves finger foods ◆ hold a two-handled cup and drink with assistance ◆ assist when being dressed by holding out their arms or legs ◆ imitate simple actions ◆ become distressed when separated from their principal carer.

1–2 years	Children become more aware of themselves as independent beings. They express a wide range of emotions and are able to initiate interactions. They can: ◆ recognise themselves in pictures or mirrors ◆ show intense affection to parents ◆ play by themselves and initiate their own play ◆ express negative feelings ◆ show pride at newly emerging skills ◆ imitate adult behaviour in their play ◆ be assertive ◆ enjoy being helpful.
2–3 years	At this age children are beginning to show a stronger sense of self and independence, expanding their range of self-help skills. They can: ◆ show awareness of gender identity ◆ indicate toileting needs ◆ assist to dress and undress themselves ◆ show preferences ◆ say no to requests ◆ begin to develop a picture of themselves, developing notions of being attractive, noisy, good ◆ show awareness of their own feelings and of others ◆ begin to talk about feelings ◆ experience rapid mood shifts ◆ show increased fearfulness ◆ display aggressive feelings and behaviours.
3–4 years	At this age their independence is growing. They can: ◆ share toys and begin to take turns, but will still need help doing so ◆ initiate play with others ◆ make up games ◆ increasingly play imaginatively.
4–5 years	At this age children are more aware of themselves as individuals. They can: ◆ show an early understanding of moral reasoning ◆ compare themselves to others ◆ develop friendships ◆ be aware of other people's feelings ◆ enjoy imaginative play with others.

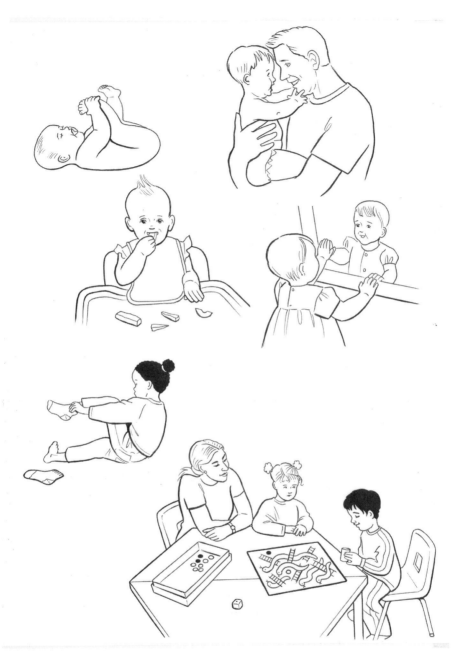

Some transitions in social and emotional development

In addition to having a sound knowledge of the emotional developmental transitions, you need to develop trusting relationships between yourself and the children. Trust is vitally important in fostering emotional intelligence. Without a trusting relationship, it is not possible for children to feel safe, secure and confident, which are all necessary for exploring and expressing feelings.

Trusting relationships between children and their principal carers start in infancy. Babies grow in confidence when they can depend on those caring for them to meet their physical and emotional care needs promptly. Settings which care for babies recognise the importance of developing firm relationships with the babies in their care by implementing the key person system to ensure continuity. A key person system links a practitioner to individual children and their parents. They have a range of responsibilities, including:

◆ sharing information with the baby's parents, including concerns, health issues and progress

◆ a settling-in process for the baby and parents

◆ developing a personal relationship with the baby and parents

◆ meeting the baby's care needs, changing nappies, feeding and settling for naps.

The key person system is discussed in Chapter 4, page 134.

This trusting relationship between babies and their care-givers needs to be maintained as they grow. In day care settings, this can be achieved through continuing to implement the key person system across the age range in the setting. For settings that do not maintain a key person system, for example schools, nursery classes and playgroups, maintaining positive and trusting relationships with all of the early years practitioners is beneficial.

THINK ABOUT IT

Reflect on how you build trusting relationships with the children in your setting.

◆ How do you ensure that positive relationships are built with their parents?

◆ How do you think positive relationships with parents affect children's emotional development?

Regular daily routines are also helpful in developing trust in the setting. Daily patterns of play, snacks, naps and meal times enable children to predict what is going to happen next, building a sense of security. Consistent rules and continuity in the quality of care given also enables trust to be developed between children and their care-givers.

Equally important is the relationship between you and the parents of the children in your care. Relationships that are mutually positive and respectful have a positive impact on the all-round development of young children. Children who see their parents genuinely welcome in the setting are more likely to feel accepted and valued themselves. Positive relationships between parents and the setting are not only good practice but are also the focus of legislation and much research. Recent research has confirmed that young children tend to do better emotionally when their parents have a greater involvement in their child's learning, developed through the positive partnership made with the setting.

Settings need to work towards creating environments where feelings are recognised and dealt with appropriately. Occasionally, settings that emphasise a calm and quiet environment can be in danger of repressing feelings (Dowling, 2000). Children need to have the freedom to explore, witness and experience feelings if they are to become emotionally intelligent.

Children experience the same wide range of feelings as adults do. However, these are often magnified as they are not accompanied by the experience that adults have in dealing with them or understanding them. No matter how well parents and the setting provide a warm and nurturing environment, children are still going to feel sad, afraid, anxious and angry from time to time. It is your role to help children to cope with their feelings and express them in a socially acceptable way that doesn't harm others and that is age- and ability-appropriate.

Some children find it incredibly hard to express their feelings verbally and this also needs to be recognised. Young children often display their feelings, both positive and negative, through actions. It is commonplace for 2-year-olds to take a toy from another child forcefully as they do not have the skills to negotiate a turn. The setting should actively support this by sensitively guiding children to use words when they are ready to do so. In the meantime, appropriate explanation should be used. Obviously, it would be unrealistic to expect immediate understanding, but through consistent, age-appropriate explanation and support, young children can develop an understanding of their feelings.

It is very important to help children to learn how to openly acknowledge their feelings. If you deny how a child feels, whether they are in pain, cross or disappointed, you are not actively supporting their emotional development. You can support their emotional development by verbally acknowledging how the child appears to feel, for example 'I can see you're disappointed about not being able to …'. This enables the children to have a name for how they are feeling, so adding to their emotional vocabulary.

CASE STUDY:

IT DOESN'T REALLY HURT

Taidi has recently moved into the area with her mother and grandmother. She has been attending the local primary school in the reception class for four weeks and has settled in well. She has made several friends and actively engages in a wide range of activities. This is the first time she has been away from both her mother and grandmother for any length of time.

While playing outside in the sand tray, another child knocks into her while pedalling backwards on a bike. Taidi starts to cry and reports the incident to a nearby adult. The adult responds by saying, 'Never mind, it doesn't really hurt.' Taidi returns to the sand tray but doesn't engage in play.

1   How does the adult know that 'it doesn't really hurt'?

2   How do you think Taidi felt with this response?

3   If Taidi's feelings had been recognised, how do you think she may have responded differently?

4   How do you think the adult should have responded?

When feelings are acknowledged, we are helping children to identify and come to terms with how they feel. How we as adults respond to the feelings of children has an impact on the development of the skills necessary to deal with feelings. However, we must be careful not to assume we know how children feel or to project feelings onto them in a given situation, for example telling a child to brave when they are going to the dentist, implying that there is a need for them to be brave.

THINK ABOUT IT

Think of a time when you hurt yourself or were feeling ill. Did you have the opportunity to share how you were feeling with another person?

When we verbalise how we feel to a sympathetic listener, we often feel slightly better. This is even more the case when injured and the injury is acknowledged as being painful by someone else. This acknowledgement empowers us to deal with how we are feeling.

How children deal with feelings and respond to situations can vary greatly from child to child and can be different to how adults would react to the same situation. A good example of this is how children respond to bereavement and grief. As adults we often feel the need to deal with and subsequently recover from grief relatively quickly, mostly due to pressures from society. However, children do not have the same sense of urgency (Woolfson, 1998). Children often take time to absorb this type of news, but once they have they will be ready to talk about their feelings or explore them through play. Sometimes they exhibit their distress through their behaviour, becoming aggressive or withdrawn. Some reactions can be immediate, while others can take weeks to show. We can help children to cope with their feelings by responding to them in a sympathetic and supportive manner. This may be verbal or non-verbal support.

It is also your role to teach children acceptable ways to respond to a wide range of difficult situations. Mostly we will be presented with the need to encourage children to share. It is not enough to tell children to share, they need to be shown how to. Depending on their age, they could be supported to take turns, or encouraged to divide the toys between them or helped to find a way to play together.

CASE STUDY:

TAKING TURNS AND SHARING

Emily is 3 years 4 months old. She has been attending Little Stars Day Nursery for three days a week for the last year. During this time, her confidence and independence have grown and she has developed some firm friendships. However she sometimes still finds it difficult to share.

Emily enjoys a wide range of activities at the nursery but is especially keen to play with the outdoor bikes. She is always eager to play outside and is often first to do so. On this occasion she has been absorbed in an activity inside so is not first to go outside to play. When she notices other children going outside, she joins them and runs straight over to one of the bikes which is being ridden by another child. She attempts to push him off the bike, insisting that it is her turn. When the other child refuses to hand over the bike, Emily gets upset and goes to find a grown up. The early years practitioner listens to Emily and reminds her that there is a need to share all of the toys in the nursery. She then encourages Emily to come up with a solution to the problem. They agree to use an egg timer to time the children on the bikes and to write names on the chalk board of those children waiting for a turn.

1   In what way do you think this situation has been handled well?

2   What aspects of Emily's development has the practitioner taken into account when using this strategy?

3   How will this impact positively on Emily's development?

Sometimes children who grab toys from others just want to join in their play but do not know how to join in. With the sensitive support of an adult, children can be taught this skill. Another important skill for children to learn is to consider the feelings of others. In Chapter 2, we looked at the work of **Piaget** and his ideas about children understanding different viewpoints on the same situation. It is hard for children to understand that not everyone shares the same feelings or viewpoint as them and this also has to be learnt. We can teach children these skills by modelling the sort of behaviour we expect from them. Every time we talk kindly and respectfully to children, we are teaching them how to talk kindly and respectfully to each other. We cannot expect children to treat each other respectfully if we are disrespectful towards them.

CASE STUDY:
STARTING SCHOOL

Olivia and Ayisha had been friends since starting nursery together a year ago. They are both due to start the same school next month and will be in the same class. Part of the preparation process involves both children having a visit to the school. Ayisha is very excited by the prospect of starting school and is looking forward to it. Olivia is less sure.

On the day of the visit, Ayisha is happy to be left by her father. However, Olivia is tearful and clingy with her mother. Ayisha is confused by Olivia's reaction and begins to feel unsettled too.

1   Why do you think Ayisha is confused by Olivia's reaction to the visit?

2   Why do you think Ayisha's reaction has unsettled Olivia?

3   How do you think this situation should be managed by the setting?

GOOD PRACTICE CHECKLIST

Supporting children's emotional development

◆ Positively support children to openly acknowledge their feelings, both positive and negative.

◆ Encourage children to describe how they are feeling, especially during conflict.

◆ Actively listen to children by getting down to their physical level and using eye contact.

◆ Convey warmth, respect and empathy.

◆ Encourage children to explore, make decisions and attempt challenging projects.

◆ Encourage children to work collaboratively on a range of projects and activities.

◆ Provide lots of opportunities for imaginative play where feelings and emotions can be safely expressed and explored.

Sense of self

Central to the effective development of children's emotions is the formation of a self-identity (Owen, 1997). Young children's self-identity is influenced by their surroundings. How they feel about themselves is learnt as they construct an image of themselves from the way they are treated by those around them. They pick up verbal, non-verbal and visual clues to how well they are liked and accepted. How young children see themselves has a direct link to their success as learners. **Erikson** (1950) strongly believed that the way adults respond to young children had potentially long-lasting effects on their self-image. Negative feelings of self-identity can be taken on into adulthood which in turn can have an effect on their ability to form relationships and to perform academically.

Throughout our lives we ask ourselves questions about the kind of person we are. Children look both inwards and outwards for the answers to these questions. By looking outwards, children pick up on how they are perceived by those around them. In order for children to develop a healthy sense of identity, they need to build up a positive yet realistic picture of the kind of person they are as well as the one they are becoming. It is your role to show continuing acceptance of the growing child in order for them to develop a positive self-image. There is a strong correlation between how children see themselves and their self-esteem.

Self-esteem

The term 'self-esteem' has become increasingly familiar when discussing children's emotional development. The development of self-esteem progresses alongside the rest of their development, which can impact on it both negatively and positively. Self-esteem is used to mean an overall evaluation of our own worth when contrasting what we believe ourselves to be with what we feel we should be. If the gap between these points is narrow then we have high self-esteem.

In the early years, children's experiences in the home and the setting begin to build the foundation of self-esteem. They develop their level of self-esteem from five main sources of information through their experiences:

- feelings of competence or lack of ability to learn
- confidence in physical skills and ability
- social acceptance
- acceptability based on behaviour
- physical appearance.

Children who develop high levels of self-esteem recognise that they are good at some things and struggle with others. They accept that they may require some help with these areas but that they are no less worthy because of it. Children with low self-esteem may develop a sense of self-dislike and find it hard to form positive relationships.

High self-esteem

A child with high self-esteem will be able to:

◆ act independently

◆ assume responsibility

◆ take pride in accomplishments

◆ tolerate frustration

◆ attempt new tasks and challenges

◆ handle positive and negative emotions

◆ offer assistance to others.

Low self-esteem

A child with low self-esteem will:

◆ avoid trying new things

◆ feel unloved and unwanted

◆ blame others for his shortcomings

◆ feel, or pretend to feel, emotionally indifferent

◆ be unable to tolerate a normal level of frustration

◆ put down his own talents and abilities

◆ be easily influenced.

Most settings provide environments that nurture children's self-esteem by forming warm relationships and supporting friendships. You can also help develop positive self-esteem by supporting children's positive disposition to learn. Ways of doing this are shown in the table below.

Supporting children's positive disposition to learn

Disposition	How to support
Curiosity and the wish to find out and explore	Provide a range of stimulating and inspiring experiences based on children's own interests
Desire to become competent	Provide appropriate praise and encouragement
Motivation to keep trying	Provide a range of problem-solving activities which are supported by adult praise and encouragement
Sense of satisfaction	Encourage and celebrate success

Encouraging and celebrating success is a very valuable means of promoting self-esteem. It can be applied to all children, no matter how small their success, as long as it is significant. However it is important not to trivialise it by praising insignificant achievements, as this can have a negative effect. Take time to get to know the children you care for. The knowledge you gather about their personalities, abilities and preference can help you to identify successes and achievement worthy of praise.

CASE STUDY:
HENRI'S LANDSCAPES

Henri is 6 years old. He is a quiet boy who has developed a few close friendships. He enjoys school, but rarely volunteers to contribute to class discussions, only doing so when prompted by the class teacher. On Monday morning, Henri arrives at school with

a bag of 'landscapes' that he has made out of small construction bricks inspired by a natural history television programme he had seen over the weekend. He asks if he can show them to the class but is told that there would not be time to do so that day.

1 How important was it to Henri to share the 'landscapes', do you think?

2 What impact do you think this missed opportunity may have on Henri's disposition to learn?

3 Why was this a success for Henri that should have been celebrated?

4 How could this situation have been handled differently?

Coping with feelings

Young children need to experience a range of emotions before they are able to begin to make sense of them. As we have already discussed, it is vital for young children to be in environments that support and encourage the exploration of feelings and emotions. It is good practice to allow children to say how they feel and to encourage them to explore these feelings in a productive way. By identifying and acknowledging feelings, we can begin to enable young children to develop the skills needed to do this.

Most settings already create environments that enable children's feelings to be stimulated by a range of activities. These activities include:

◆ *listening to music* – to move to music, join in singing and express themselves through the use of musical instruments

◆ *playing with dough and other tactile and malleable materials* – enables children to release tension and negative energy as they manipulate them; they may also find some tactile materials soothing

◆ *role play opportunities* – to explore feelings and emotions through their play, resulting in a better understanding of their feelings.

Children's feelings can be stimulated by a range of activities

If children are given the opportunity to talk about the feelings stirred through these types of play, they will be able to identify these feelings in other situations. Likewise, they will be able to identify negative feelings too. If you take the opportunity to help children to identify patterns in their feelings, they will begin to be able to regulate their emotions. Emotional regulation enables children to direct their emotions appropriately.

CASE STUDY:

DEATH OF A PET

Archie is 4 years 5 months. He attends nursery for five afternoons a week and is a happy confident boy who enjoys the company of other children. While playing in the sand, the early years practitioner notices that he repeatedly buries a plastic dog and digs it up again. The practitioner asks Archie what he is doing. Archie explains that when you die you get buried.

The practitioner stays with Archie, observing his play and allows him to talk about what he is doing. Eventually he tells the practitioner that his dog died a few days ago as it was very old. The practitioner encourages Archie to talk about how he feels and all the special things he can remember about his dog. Through a later discussion with Archie's father, the practitioner discovers this is his first experience of bereavement.

1 In what way do you think this situation has been handled well?

2 What additional strategies could be used to support Archie?

3 How will having the support to deal with his feelings on this occasion support him next time he experiences bereavement?

To help children explore their emotions, you can use a range of resources, including:

◆ *books* – there is a wide range of books available especially designed to help children to deal with a variety of situations and resulting feelings. Additional props and resources can be added to story books to encourage children to act out situations using the book, giving them the opportunity to explore their feelings

◆ *circle time* – this provides the ideal group listening system for enhancing children's self-esteem, promoting moral values and discussing feelings. It is a democratic system that involves all children, giving them equal rights and opportunities. Circle time supports children's emotional development by providing a practical opportunity to discuss concerns and explore solutions.

However, it is important to allow children the right to not take part as some children find this form of activity uncomfortable

◆ *puppets* – these are good tools for teaching children how to respond to difficult situations. You can involve the children in puppet shows which focus on the possible problems they may have dealing with other children. Puppets can enable children to explore feelings or to express concerns

◆ *music* – love, respect and appreciation for music are easy to share with children and build life skills at the same time. During the early years, musical skills help to build self-esteem and enhance expression.

All of the resources outlined above provide valuable opportunities for children to learn to cope with their feelings. Children are able to display both negative and positive feelings. Working with puppets can be especially useful as a means of exploring children's emotional development. **Denham** (1986) noticed from observations of children at play that those who displayed both negative and positive emotions in play were more able to recognise and comprehend other children's feelings. You need to value play opportunities that allow children to explore their emotions in this way and look at approaches that enable you to support them.

How adults interact with children

Gottman's (1997) research on how parents dealt with emotional behaviour within the family identified four different parenting styles of approach, as shown in the table below.

Parenting styles of approach to dealing with emotional behaviour

Style of approach	Characteristics
A critical approach	Parents actively criticised children for showing negative emotions
A dismissive approach	Parents ignore or trivialise children's negative emotions
Laissez-faire approach	Parents accept children's negative emotions but fail to provide guidance or support
Supportive approach	Parents accept children's negative emotions, acknowledging them and demonstrating understanding

Source: Gottman (1997)

Although these approaches apply to parents, they can also be applied to anyone caring for young children. Parents and carers who take an active role in supporting negative feelings through emotional coaching enable children to understand and control their own feelings and to develop empathy with others. **Goleman** (1998) recognised the process of emotional coaching through his studies of successful parent–child interactions, identifying five elements to the process.

1 Become aware of children's emotions.

2 Recognise the emotion as an opportunity for intimacy and teaching.

3 Listen empathetically, validating children's feelings.

4 Help children find words to label the emotion they are experiencing.

5 Set limits while exploring strategies to solve the problem.

Through his research, **Goleman** noticed that children who experience emotional coaching:

◆ are physically healthier

◆ do better academically

◆ are more able to sustain friendships

◆ have fewer behaviour problems

◆ are less violent.

Although they still experience sadness, anger and are scared at times, he noted that they are better able to comfort themselves and recover to carry on with productive activities. He concluded that these children have higher levels of emotional health and are therefore more emotionally intelligent.

TRY IT OUT

Take time to observe the children in your setting. Focus on the adult interactions during times when strong emotions are being expressed by children.

◆ *Using **Gottman**'s styles of approach, identify which approach is being most used.*

◆ *To what extent can you see the emotional coaching approach in practice?*

◆ *Reflect on the practice you observe and discuss your findings with your colleagues.*

Key theories about how children feel

John Bowlby

John Bowlby's theories on attachment were introduced in Chapter 4. Attachment is a positive emotional link between babies and young children and their parents or other key carers. It refers to the child's part of the relationship as opposed to the term 'bonding' which refers to the care-giver's part. The formation of children's first emotional relationship, usually with the mother, is considered to be one of the most important achievements of childhood. This relationship lays the foundation for future confidence and security and, if broken, can cause a considerable amount of trauma.

Bowlby's attachment theory and its impact on early relationships is discussed in Chapter 4, page 119.

Impact on current practice

Sleeping baby

Bowlby's work contributed to changes in services for children. Nurseries that had provided full-time care for children of mothers who worked during the war became part-time, creating more nursery spaces and job opportunities for the returning soldiers.

It is from **Bowlby**'s work that further research showed the effects of separation from parents on children when hospitalised. This research was instrumental in making it possible for parents to stay with their children in hospital.

The main positive outcomes of good attachment experience in the early years seem to be mostly social:

◆ self-confidence

◆ self-esteem

◆ the ability to care for others and to be cared for.

Settings that value the importance of children's attachments, at home and in the setting, develop strong working relationships with the families of the children they care for. They make time to get to know individual children's needs and interests. They implement strategies that recognise the possible anxiety that may be caused when children are separated from their attachment figure. These include the key person system and the settling-in process, which supports a smooth transition from home to setting when starting or moving on to another class or setting.

Bowlby's attachment theory highlights the trauma babies may experience when they become separated from their attachment figure. He believed that separation anxiety could have a serious effect on cognitive, social and emotional development. You can support babies and young children at times of separation by firstly being familiar with how children react at different ages and stages of their development.

Separation anxiety usually emerges around 9 months of age and generally peaks between 12 and 24 months. Separation anxiety is usually expressed by crying or becoming withdrawn. Babies more commonly show separation anxiety through crying and in two different scenarios:

- The baby cries when they are left because they fear the parent will not return and they cry when the parent does return because it reminds them of how it felt when they left the first time.

- Separation anxiety can also occur in the home. The baby may become anxious and cry because the parent is not physically close to the baby. This can still occur even when it was the baby that crawled away.

Between the ages of 2 and 3 years, separation anxiety begins to decrease. At this stage, children tend to separate easily especially if they are being left with a familiar person. Between the age of 3 and 4, most children will separate confidently, often forgetting to wave goodbye unless reminded.

Sigmund Freud

Sigmund Freud (1856–1939)

Sigmund Freud believed that most people who were regarded as severely disturbed were really suffering from a variety of mental disorders. This led him to develop psychoanalysis, which consisted of various theories about human behaviour. His work subsequently diversified with theoretical approaches that focused on the impact of personality and conflict on children's development. Like **Piaget**, **Freud** saw development in definite stages that everyone shares within childhood, but the focus of his theory was the role of conscious and unconscious thoughts. According to **Freud**, development occurs when we struggle to balance the demands of:

- the id – the motivational, instinctive, pleasure-seeking part of personality
- the ego – conscious thinking, prevents anti-social behaviour
- the super-ego – deals with moral issues.

Freud believed the super-ego to be divided into two parts: the conscience and the ego-ideal. Our conscience makes us feel guilty or ashamed when we have behaved badly, whereas our ego-ideal makes us feel proud of ourselves when we have avoided temptation and behaved well. **Freud** suggested that at the age of 5 or 6 the super-ego starts to develop, resulting in boys developing a sexual desire for their mothers, leading to intense rivalry with their fathers. He called this the Oedipus complex. He believed that this led to boys of this age feeling frightened as they are much weaker than their fathers. This stage of development eventually moves on when boys go through the process of identification in which they take on the moral values of the same-sexed parent and this leads to the formation of the super-ego.

Freud also believed that a similar process happened to girls at about the same age. They develop an Electra complex based on their desire for their fathers. Girls also move through the process of identification when they take on the moral values of their mothers. **Freud** claimed that girls do not identify as strongly with their mothers as boys do with their fathers, resulting in a weaker super-ego being developed.

Impact on current practice

The main impact of **Freud**'s thinking on settings is that children must be supported in working through their emotional or psychological crises in order to develop a sense of emotional well-being. This is mainly achieved through providing children with a balanced range of play opportunities, providing art materials and opportunities for role play. The importance of providing these types of play opportunities is discussed in more detail in Chapter 6.

THINK ABOUT IT

Using your knowledge of **Freud**'s theory of the id, the ego and the super-ego, consider the children you work with.

Can you relate these areas of **Freud**'s thinking to the children's behaviour?

Other aspects of common practice in settings can also be linked to **Freud**'s theory. These include how we develop and build relationships with the children we care for, as well as how we support them emotionally in the setting. We have discussed these areas of practice in more detail earlier in the chapter.

Carl Rogers

Carl Rogers (1902–87)

Carl Rogers was an American psychologist who is probably best known as the founder of 'client-centred' therapy. However, he had much to contribute to education. He believed in a humanistic approach that looked at both personality and behaviour. He identified that everyone has the potential to develop into healthy, well-adjusted adults but in order to do so needs unconditional positive regard from the adults around them and positive self-regard from themselves. Unconditional positive regard does not mean that we never discipline children or demonstrate disappointment. Instead it means we care for them without judgement.

According to **Rogers**, the concept of self is of central importance. He believed that an individual's self-concept is mainly conscious, consisting of our thoughts and feelings about ourselves both as individuals and in relation to others. Within **Rogers'** theory, there are two selves:

◆ self-concept – the self as it is currently

◆ ideal self – the self-concept that an individual would most like to have.

The smaller the gap between the self-concept and the ideal self the higher the self-esteem. However, people experience problems when the gap between the two is too wide: for example, a child who thinks they are good at sharing but find themselves being asked to share a piece of equipment they want for themselves. This is often met with either justification for not sharing (distortion) or denial that the event ever took place. Both distortion and denial both fail to address the gap between the self-image and the ideal self, therefore making the child more vulnerable and anxious.

CASE STUDY:
TOBY'S STICKY PROBLEM

At Green Park Pre-School, a group of 3-year-olds are gathered around the painting table. They are working on a collaborative piece of collage work that is to be displayed in the hallway. There are plenty of resources for all of the children to participate in the activity at the same time.

Toby snatches a glue spreader from the child standing next to him who begins to cry. 'It's mine anyway,' says Toby attempting to justify his actions. Owen, the early years practitioner, intervenes and asks Toby to give the glue spreader back while he helps him to find his own. 'It's not kind to snatch things from other people. You need to ask if you can borrow it or for help to find your own.' Toby returns the glue spreader and finds his own. Both children continue happily with the activity.

1 How well do you feel this incident was handled by the practitioner?

2 Why didn't Owen tell Toby that he was unkind for snatching the glue stick?

3 What impact do you think this incident had on Toby's self-image?

THINK ABOUT IT

Think about **Rogers'** ideas about self-concept and ideal self.

◆ How can you help to minimise the gap between the two?

◆ How do **Rogers'** theories link to the formation of positive self-esteem as discussed earlier in this chapter?

Rogers also valued the relationship between children and their teachers and care-givers as a crucial influence on the learning experience of young children. He identified the qualities and attitudes in the table below as necessary to facilitate positive learning experiences.

Facilitating positive learning experiences

What	How	Why
Genuineness	Communicating with and responding to children in a way that conveys genuine pleasure in a non-judgmental way	Genuine pleasure with children's achievement or behaviour has more impact than if these feelings are not really felt.
Acceptance	Valuing children as individuals and all aspects of their personalities with their thoughts and opinions respected	Children who feel accepted and liked by those around them have higher self-esteem which impacts positively on their ability to learn.
Empathy	Showing understanding of children's experience in the setting from their point of view	Enables practitioners to ensure a high-quality learning experience for all children.

Summary

The theorists discussed in this chapter all focus on the importance of emotional development. They emphasise the importance of young children's emotional development receiving the same level of recognition and attention as all other areas of their development. The chapter has considered the importance of supporting young children's emotional development, how this can be achieved and the long-term benefits of doing so. In addition to these key points, your role as an early years practitioner has also been highlighted as vital in ensuring the setting supports the exploration of feelings and emotions in a positive and safe environment. Feelings need to be recognised and dealt with appropriately in order to encourage emotional health. Emotions affect our social behaviour and influence the choices we make. Learning to manage feelings and emotions can be difficult for many children and can result in later psychological difficulties if not appropriately supported early on by the around adults.

The chapter also addresses the value of high-quality relationships between children and practitioners and between practitioners and parents, identifying the impact of supporting positive dispositions to learning. This, along with the children having the opportunity to freely explore, witness and experience feelings, enables early years practitioners to ensure that they become emotionally intelligent and successful learners.

CHECK YOUR UNDERSTANDING

1 What resources and materials would you provide in order to stimulate emotions?

2 What resources and materials would you provide in order ensure children have the opportunity to explore their feelings?

3 How can early years practitioners support positive dispositions to learning?

4 What impact does emotional coaching have on children who are displaying negative feelings?

References and further reading

Denham, S. (1986) 'Social cognition, social behaviour and emotion in pre-schoolers', *Child Development*, Vol. 57, pp 194–201

Dowling, M. (2000) *Young Children's Personal, Social and Emotional Development*, Paul Chapman Publications

Dunn, J. (1993) *Young Children's Close Relationships Beyond Attachment*, Sage

Elfer, P., Goldschmeid, E. and Selleck, D. (2003) *Key Person in the Nursery: Building relationships for quality provision*, David Fulton

Erikson, E. (1950) *Childhood and Society*, Penguin

Gardner, H. (1983) *Frames of Mind: The theory of multiple intelligences*, Basic Books

Goleman, D. (1996) *Emotional Intelligence: Why it matters more than IQ*, Bloomsbury

Goleman, D. (1998) *Working with emotional intelligence*, Bloomsbury

Gottman, J. and Declaire, J. (1997) *The Heart of Parenting: How to raise an emotionally intelligent child*, Bloomsbury

Macintyre, C. (2002) *Enhancing Learning Through Play*, David Fulton

Maslow, A.H. (1962) *Towards a Psychology of Being*, Van Nostrand

Owen, P. (1997) *Early Childhood Education and Care*, Trentham Books

Pascal, C. and Bertram, T. (1997) *Effective Early Learning: Case studies in improvement*, Hodder & Stoughton

Pound, L. (2005) *How Children Learn*, Practical Pre-School series, Step Forward Publishing

Roberts, R. (1995) *Self-Esteem and Successful Early Learning*, Hodder & Stoughton

Schaffer, H. Rudolf (1998) *Making Decisions about Children*, Blackwell

Woolfson, R. (1998) *From Birth to Starting School*, Caring Books

Chapter 6

Children's play

Introduction

It is essential that early years practitioners understand and value children's play. One of the greatest attributes of play is that it allows children to learn through trial and error, while making connections with previous learning and transferring knowledge and understanding from one area of play to another. Play provides children with the non-threatening opportunity to explore new experiences with no right or wrong way of doing so.

Play supports both learning and practice yet how truly valued is play among all professionals working with children? In some settings, play is often reserved as an activity to occupy or reward children when they have finished work, rather than a vehicle for learning in its own right. It is a sad fact that children in school are particularly vulnerable to diminishing play opportunities as more formal teaching takes priority in order to meet academic targets. However, over recent years, the benefits of young children learning through play have been recognised with the development of Foundation Stage units where the majority of learning takes place through child-initiated play or adult-initiated play. Children's learning is encouraged through play and not at the expense of play.

Children today are growing up in a society where they have:

◆ much less freedom to play outside
◆ less opportunity to socialise and play with other children away from an adult
◆ less opportunity to play in mixed-age groups
◆ more visual input from television and computer games.

Settings are familiar with redressing the balance for those children who are experiencing an inadequate variety of play opportunities, usually due to an excessive amount of one type of play. Traditionally this has been computer games and television. However, there is another group of children who also experience a lack of opportunity to play – those with an over-organised way of life. Today many children attend organised and structured extra-curricular activities in a bid to widen their experiences and develop skills, but this is often at the expense of child-initiated play. These children have very little opportunity to 'just play' due to their busy lifestyles.

In order to provide children with the best possible play opportunities, it is helpful to understand the different types of play, where some of the theories of play come from and how most of these theories have influenced and informed our practice. By understanding a range of theories and philosophies about play, you can anticipate how children may behave or react. You can analyse and make sense of observations, which in turn enable you to plan appropriately for the children in your setting. However, it is important to remain objective and keep an open mind when applying theory to practice.

This chapter covers:

◆ The pioneers of the early years curriculum
◆ Tina Bruce and free-flow play
◆ Pulling the theories together
◆ Adult-initiated play and child-initiated play
◆ Structured play
◆ The play environment
◆ Heuristic play
◆ Outdoor play.

The theorists and researchers covered in this chapter are:
◆ **Friedrich Froebel**, page 168
◆ **Lev Vygotsky**, page 173
◆ **Susan Isaacs**, page 173
◆ **Maria Montessori**, page 175
◆ **B.F. Skinner**, page 176
◆ **Margaret McMillan**, page 176
◆ **Tina Bruce**, page 177
◆ **Jerome Bruner**, page 185
◆ **Jean Piaget**, page 185
◆ **Elinor Goldschmeid**, page 194.

The pioneers of the early years curriculum

Friedrich Froebel

Friedrich Froebel made childhood play a subject of study. Through his study, he identified the impact play has on young children's development and learning. By observing young children at play, he concluded that play was of central importance in his philosophy for the education and care of young children. He developed a curriculum around the child's free play which he came to believe was the highest form of learning.

Friedrich Froebel (1782–1852)

Froebel believed that teachers should not teach by rote, which was common at the time, but by encouraging self-expression through play. He valued play and the outdoor environment highly, believing that both space and light were essential for learning. Froebel-styled kindergartens encouraged children to make full use of the outside play environment. **Froebel** considered free-flow play to be something all children shared in common and that by seeing each child as an individual, early years practitioners could provide appropriate and sensitive help in order to support development and learning. He identified free-flow play as play that children were fully engaged in and in control of, that had many features and that was rich in learning possibilities. **Tina Bruce** (1991) clearly defines these features describing them as a network of related processes.

Bruce's ideas are discussed in more detail on page 177 of this chapter.

Froebel's work raised the status of play significantly across Europe and parts of the USA, with large numbers of kindergartens offering provision based on his work. He has greatly influenced practice today with the current early years curriculum using play as a focus and key vehicle for learning.

Froebel believed that through different types of play children could experiment with resources and materials, develop an understanding of how things work, use their imaginations, be creative and act out experiences. To enable children to fully benefit from all of these possibilities, it is essential that you provide time and the resources and be available to extend activities and, therefore, learning.

The table below defines the types of play **Froebel** believed to be valuable and gives examples of the areas in your setting where you might see this type of play in action.

Types of play and their possibilities for learning

Type of play	Example	Area of play
Experiment	◆ How things work ◆ Cause and effect ◆ Different properties of materials ◆ The different sounds that can be made from different materials ◆ How to plan out tasks	Creative area, interest table, music area, sand and water play, construction area, outdoor play
Understand	◆ The roles and responsibilities people in the community have ◆ Different reactions to situations from different children ◆ That different people have different views, opinions and expectations	Citizenship, PSHE, circle time, planned visits from people in the community, imaginative play, role play, outdoor play
Imagine	◆ New situations and scenarios ◆ How stories could end ◆ How others might feel in their role	Stories, imaginative play, role play, small world play, outdoor play
Create	Models, patterns, dances, musical pieces, pieces of art work	Art area, creative area, music area, movement to music, outdoor play
Act out	Personal concerns or anxieties	Imaginative play, role play area, small world play, outdoor play

You will have noticed that some of these types of play can be seen in more than one area. Settings which provide a broad range of experiences that cover all of these areas of play are more likely to connect with a wider number of children in the setting, therefore maximising overall learning potential. You will have also noticed that the outdoor environment features highly, covering all areas. **Froebel** saw the garden as the best environment for young children's learning and development.

THINK ABOUT IT

Using your knowledge of **Froebel**'s philosophy on play consider the children that you work with.

- Do the play opportunities and experiences that you provide reflect **Froebel**'s work?
- In which areas of play do you think you are more likely to see evidence of **Froebel**'s philosophy in action?
- How do you know you are meeting the learning needs of all of the children?

Froebel pioneered the view that play is the highest level of learning, a function that allows children to apply their knowledge and understanding – bringing together what they know, understand and feel. He recognised play as a means of allowing children to think flexibly, adapting what they know and trying out different possibilities. He believed that children should be engaged in their own learning rather than being shown or told how to do things. He believed that play provides children with the opportunity to problem-solve using previously learnt skills and past experience to apply to new problems.

CASE STUDY:
TEAM WORK AND PROBLEM-SOLVING

Frankie, Rory, Ned and Gracie are aged between 3½ and 4 years old. They attend nursery five mornings a week and often play together. They especially like to play in the sand.

Today they are using cardboard tubes to make tunnels and roadways in the sand. They have a collection of cars and lorries as well as farm animals to play with. A car gets stuck in one of the longer tubes. The children discuss how they are going to solve the problem. Frankie suggests tipping the tube up but the car doesn't move. Ned gets a wooden spoon from the imaginative play area and uses the handle to try and push the car out but the spoon does not reach. Finally Gracie holds the tube up over the sand tray and pats it firmly with the palm of her hand. The car falls out of the tube into the sand.

➡

1 How did the children know to apply these different strategies to solve the problem?

2 Identify the types of activities and experiences the children may have gained these skills from.

3 Have you witnessed children in your setting applying problem-solving strategies learnt from one area of play to another?

TRY IT OUT

Observe the children at play and specifically look for any problem-solving strategies that they use. Observe the way they approach the problem and try to solve it. Can you identify if this skill has been developed in the setting? Which activities and experience provided in the setting have helped the child to develop these skills?

GOOD PRACTICE CHECKLIST

Opportunities provided by play

The curriculum in your setting should provide play opportunities for children to:

◆ develop their independence

◆ problem-solve

◆ use their imagination

◆ experiment

◆ adapt ideas

◆ engage in own learning

◆ select materials from a wide range of resources

◆ actively interact with their surroundings

◆ be self-motivated

◆ be observed during child-initiated play

◆ play alone and with other children.

Froebel's influence on Forest Schools is discussed in Chapter 1, page 37.

Lev Vygotsky

Lev Vygotsky's work was very similar to aspects of **Froebel**. He considered play to be a crucial element in development, recognising that children learned through social relationships and interactions. He saw play as creating a zone of proximal development in which children functioned at a higher level than they did during everyday tasks. He believed that both adults and more skilled children can nurture this learning by supporting, explaining and extending the experience further.

In contrast to **Froebel**'s theory that children should engage in their own learning, **Vygotsky** believed that what a child could do with support today, he can do alone tomorrow (Vygotsky, 1978). **Vygotsky** (1978), **Bruner** (1976) and **Moyles** (1999) all recognised the impact play has on children's social competence. They valued the practitioner as instrumental in enabling young children to expand and apply their knowledge.

Vygotsky's theories are also discussed in the following chapters:

◆ Chapter 2, How children learn, page 58

◆ Chapter 3, Children's communication, page 78

◆ Chapter 4, Children's relationships, page 110.

Bruner's theories are discussed in the following chapters:

◆ Chapter 2, How children learn, page 62

◆ Chapter 3, Children's communication, pages 79 and 93

◆ Chapter 4, Children's relationships, page 113.

Susan Isaacs

Susan Isaacs studied philosophy at Manchester University followed by psychology at Newnham College, Cambridge. She was especially interested in children's play, identifying its importance in their development. Her pioneering research was theoretical in nature, bridging philosophy, psychology and psychoanalysis. Much of her philosophy was based on meticulous records and observation of children aged 2–9 years in the naturalistic setting where she worked. These allowed her to reflect on children's learning and development, building a framework from which she worked. She saw children as active learners. She believed that through play and with gentle guidance and support children could make sense of the world around them. **Isaacs** recognised the value of imaginative play and believed that this form of play should be valued and encouraged by those working with young children. She also recognised the value of the outdoor play environment, as had **Froebel**, and encouraged the children to make good use of outdoor space in developing exploration and enquiry.

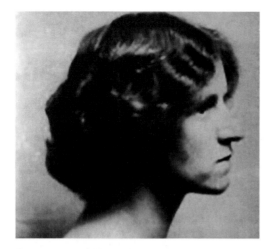

Susan Isaacs (1885–1948)

Isaacs was also interested in young children's emotional development. She recognised the impact play had on children's emotional development, helping them to deal with fears and empathise with others. She also recognised the impact poor treatment from adults could have on their emotional development, concluding that adults should interact with young children in a positive and respectful way, avoiding being sarcastic or breaking promises, but answering their questions in a sensitive manner.

Children's self-directed play and learning was prioritised, with minimum of interference from adults. The role of the adult was essentially to observe the children and to identify their needs and interests and to plan a suitable curriculum accordingly. Much of **Isaacs**' early years philosophy was based on **Froebel**'s theory of learning through doing. The three key points to her philosophy included:

♦ an emphasis on curiosity and exploration play

♦ the use and development of language to promote thinking

♦ great attention paid to children's emotional development.

In contrast to **Bruner**'s theory of scaffolding learning, enabling children to move on to the next stage (discussed in Chapter 2), **Isaacs** believed that quiet, positive encouragement, showing children what to do and how to do it, was far more effective. Her work had a huge impact on the educational world during the late 1920s and 1930s.

THINK ABOUT IT

Using your knowledge of **Isaacs**' philosophy on play, consider the children that you work with.

♦ How do the early years practitioners support and encourage children during play experiences?

♦ Does the way they communicate reflect **Isaacs**' work?

Isaac's influence on Forest Schools is discussed in Chapter 1, page 37.

Maria Montessori

Maria Montessori was introduced in Chapter 1.

Through intensive observations of many children, **Montessori** concluded that children learn best through using their senses, which she believed should be developed prior to intellect. She believed that children learn through movement, particularly the movement of the hand which she identified as being linked to intellectual and cognitive development. From her observations, she also concluded that very young children are able to learn to read, write and count. However, she believed this should only be taught when they begin to show an interest in these skills.

Montessori identified particularly sensitive periods of time when children were especially keen to learn. She believed that children have these sensitive periods when their senses are ready to learn new ideas and that early years practitioners should be able to identify these times in a child's development. Much of the Montessori curriculum is focused on the use of the five senses, with activities being carefully planned to maximise their use. Activities are presented with the opportunity to:

◆ use all the senses, not just sight and hearing

◆ include outdoor as well as indoor activities

◆ explore on their own without direction.

The Montessori curriculum in nurseries today is based on **Montessori**'s principles of education. It aims to support all aspects of children's personal and social development and is divided into the curriculum areas listed in the table in Chapter 1, page 18.

Practitioners working in Montessori schools claim that the approach promotes all-round development and leads children to being independent, confident decision-makers. However, critics believe it can lack academic input and it focuses on daily living skills. **Montessori** recognised the impact the learning environment could have on children. Many of the teaching resources she used were specially designed for her approach and she recommended that furniture should be child-sized and allow children to freely select resources and equipment, a concept evident in all early years settings and schools today. In settings following a Montessori approach, play is recognised as being the main vehicle for learning and children are given the opportunity to have long periods of uninterrupted play. The early years practitioner will follow the child's lead during play and encourage the use of their senses to explore and discover.

LEARNING IN A MONTESSORI PRE-SCHOOL

It is early spring and a small group of children at the Montessori pre-school are enjoying being in the garden. They are with an adult looking at the snowdrops and crocuses that are in flower. The children had planted the bulbs in the autumn. The adult encourages the children to look carefully at the flowers and to draw pictures of them. One of the children smells the snowdrops and comments on them not having a smell. The adult asks the other children in the group if they would like to smell the snowdrops and if they think they smell.

1 How is this adult encouraging the children to discover through their senses?

2 Do you feel this adult is leading the children or following the children's lead?

3 How do you encourage the children in your setting to explore through their senses?

4 Can you think of a time when you followed the lead of the children during an activity? Did you learn anything from this situation?

For more about **Maria Montessori**, see Chapter 1, pages 15–21.

B.F. Skinner

Skinner is best known for his behaviourist theory which he developed through experiments on rodents and applied to children. He believed that behaviour is learned and that it could be influenced. He regarded play as a means of rewarding children after periods of learning rather than a means of learning. Although his operant conditioning theory has been applied to behaviour modification techniques which are widely used today, his views on play are less highly regarded.

Skinner is also discussed in Chapter 3, page 75.

Margaret McMillan

Margaret McMillan (1860–1931)

In 1923 **Margaret McMillan** was elected president of the Nursery Schools Association. Her work had focused on the health and well-being of young children from deprived and disadvantaged families. She established nurseries that provided a mix of care and education. Her settings established regular routines for meal times and sleep as well as outdoor play. She believed that children were ill prepared for school because of the lack of recognition for early years provision. **McMillan's** educational philosophy drew on **Froebel**'s theory and also placed a great emphasis on free play and the outdoor environment. The overall approach adopted by **McMillan** was seen as exemplary and not only influenced the building designs of nursery schools, but also helped to establish the school medical service and the school meal service which we are familiar with today.

McMillan's influence on Forest Schools is discussed in Chapter 1, page 37.

Tina Bruce and free-flow play

Tina Bruce is a leading expert in early childhood education in the UK. She places a strong emphasis on the benefits of play in preparing children to take their place in society. She identifies play as vital in early years education and recognises the contribution play makes to children's social competence. She has questioned whether children's right to play is being denied by the increasing emphasis on formal education in the early years (Bruce, 2001).

Based on her research, **Bruce** has identified free-flow play, describing it as a network of related processes which include struggle, exploration, manipulation, discovery and practice, all catalysts to children's development. Free-flow play arises out of 12 features of play which have been identified as important in its development (see below). When these features are considered together, it is possible to assess whether play is of sufficient quality to be called free-flow play.

Twelve features of free-flow play

1 It is an active process without an end product. Play experiences and activities are beneficial in their own right and do not need to have an end product, for example a painting or model, to make it a worthwhile learning experience.

2 It is intrinsically motivated. Children are motivated to take part in an activity or experience by their natural curiosity.

3 It exerts no external pressure to conform to rules, pressures, goals tasks or definite direction. There is no right or wrong way of doing it.

4 It is about possible, alternative worlds, which involve 'supposing' and 'what if' which lift players to their highest levels of functioning. This involves being imaginative, creative, original and innovative.

5 It is about participants becoming fully absorbed in ideas, feelings and relationships. It involves reflection on and becoming aware of what we know.

6 It actively uses previous first-hand experiences, including struggle, manipulation, exploration, discovery and practice. Children can use past experience to develop new and existing skills.

7 It is sustained and, when in full flow, helps us to function in advance of what we can actually do in our real lives. It is similar to **Vygotsky**'s idea that children are able to function at a higher level during play than during everyday tasks.

8 During free-flow play, we use the technical prowess, mastery and competence we have previously developed and so can be in control.

9 It can be initiated by a child or an adult, but if by an adult they must pay particular attention to features 3, 5 and 11.

10 It can be solitary. Children can still experience high-quality play even if playing alone.

11 It can be in partnership, or groups of adults and/or children who will be sensitive to each other.

12 It is an integrating mechanism which brings together everything we learn, know, feel and understand.

Source: Adapted from Bruce (1991)

When children free-flow play they are able to reach their deepest and widest levels of learning. Play is not just about learning new skills but is also about using established skills in a flexible and imaginative way. It is from **Froebel**'s work in addition to **Montessori** and **Steiner** (see Chapter 1, page 21) that **Bruce** identified ten principles of play (see below).

Ten principles of play

1 Childhood is seen as valid in itself, as part of life and not simply as preparation for adulthood. It is current, not just practice for the future.

2 The whole child is considered to be important: health, physical, emotional, social, intellectual and spiritual development.

3 Learning is not compartmentalised, everything is linked.

4 Intrinsic motivation, resulting in child-initiated self-directed activity is valued.

5 Self-discipline is emphasised.

6 There are especially receptive periods of learning at different stages of development.

7 What children can do is the starting point in the child's education.

8 There is an inner structure in the child which includes the imagination and which emerges especially under favourable conditions.

9 The people with whom the child has contact are of central importance.

10 The child's education is seen as an interaction between the child and the environment.

Source: Bruce (1987)

The ten principles provide practitioners with a useful framework to follow when planning and implementing their early years curricula. In addition to the above features of free-flow play and principles of play, **Bruce** also describes 12 features of play (see below) from which she feels free-flow play arises. When the features are considered together it is possible to assess the quality of the free-flow play in a setting. If all 12 features are present, we can be more confident that we are observing free-flow play in action than if only a few are present.

Twelve features of play

1   In their play, children use the first-hand experiences that they have in life.

2   Children make up rules as they play, and so keep control of their play.

3   Children make play props.

4   Children choose to play. They cannot be made to play.

5   Children rehearse the future in their role play.

6   Children pretend when they play.

7   Children play alone sometimes.

8   Children and/or adults play together, in parallel, associatively, co-operatively in pairs or groups.

9   Each player has a personal play agenda, although they may not be aware of this.

10 Children playing will be deeply involved, and difficult to distract from their deep learning.

11 Children try out their most recent learning, skills and competencies when they play.

12 Children at play co-ordinate their ideas, feelings and make sense of relationships. When play is co-ordinated it flows along in a sustained way. It is called free-flow play.

Source: Bruce (2001)

Bruce is also discussed in the following chapters:

◆ Chapter 2, How children learn, page 57

◆ Chapter 3, Children's communication, page 85.

Pulling the theories together

You will have recognised many aspects of your own practice from the philosophies and theories of the pioneers of early education discussed in this chapter. Their ideas have been highly influential in the formulation of current day early years programmes and frameworks. The Curriculum Guidance for the Foundation Stage (discussed in Chapter 1, page 2) states that play needs time and space, drawing on many of the philosophies outlined above.

When we look closely at these theories and philosophies, we can see that the majority of them have aspects in common.

- They are based on years of meticulous observation, which have been invaluable in identifying the learning needs of young children.
- They recognise the value of play and the impact it has on children's learning.
- They recognise the importance of the role of the adult in facilitating, supporting and extending learning.

There is consistent agreement amongst these theories that the role of the adult is to:

- support and respond to children's needs, recognising their potential
- support children's skills as players and learners
- enrich children's play
- support children's ideas, extending them with additional ideas and resources
- enable children to develop their own play through chosen themes
- interact in a sensitive and respectful way, valuing children's ideas and contributions.

These theories and philosophies can be categorised into the viewpoints given in the table below.

Viewpoints on play

Viewpoints	Theory
The romantic viewpoint Children's development and learning is regarded as holistic and play is seen as integral to childhood. Children are happy when playing and playing is learning.	Linked to **Froebel**'s theory on play
The behaviourist viewpoint Play is used as a reward after periods of learning.	Linked to **Skinner**'s theory of operant conditioning
The therapeutic viewpoint Play is regarded as a means of supporting young children's emotional development.	Linked to **Isaacs**' theory
The cognitive viewpoint Play is recognised as a means by which children develop a range of skills: communications, problem-solving, understanding of social rules.	Linked to **Froebel**'s and **Vygotsky**'s theories
The biological viewpoint Play is recognised as a means of supporting the development of creativity and imagination which is essential to the development of the human brain.	Scientists and psychologist have concluded that, as playing is something all humans can do, it must have a biological function

When we consider these various viewpoints of play, we can see that it involves choice, space and time. Some viewpoints place more value on play than others. For example, **Montessori** did not recognise the value of imaginative play. For her, play was most valuable when it was linked to real-life activities.

As outlined in this chapter, theories of play have changed over time and there are different emphases according to which viewpoint on play is taken. However, they all have similar theories on *why* children play:

◆ Play allows children to explore and express ideas, emotions and feelings. Play can be seen as emotionally therapeutic, providing a safe outlet for tension. Children have the opportunity to experience feelings, learning to cope with these more rationally.

Exploring and expressing feelings

◆ Play provides opportunities for relaxation and social contact with others.

Relaxation and social contact

◆ Play enables children to use excess energy.

Using excess energy

◆ Play enables children to practise skills, preparing them for the next stage in their development.

Practising skills

Problem-solving

◆ Play challenges children's problem-solving skills, developing their cognitive, manipulative and social skills which contribute to their all-round intellectual growth.

Perseverance and self-confidence

◆ Play enables children to master learning through developing perseverance, social interactions, self-esteem and self-confidence.

It has been recognised that high-quality play experiences during the early years give children a solid foundation for later learning. This fact has resulted in the Foundation Stage outlining the requirement for reception teachers to build on the same play-based curriculum that is well established in early years settings.

The following checklist can enable you to evaluate the quality of the play provision in your setting.

GOOD PRACTICE CHECKLIST

Evaluating the quality of play provision

◆ Ensure that the daily routine includes plenty of time for children to play.

◆ Be prepared to join in but not to takeover their play.

◆ Interact during play in a meaningful and sensitive way.

◆ Know when to leave children to develop their own play.

◆ Create challenging and exciting environments for play.

◆ Value the ideas, thoughts and feelings of children, encouraging their ideas for new indoor play scenarios.

◆ Observe children at play.

◆ Have the opportunity to revisit play experiences and scenarios.

◆ The possibilities for play are endless but should be based on children's own interests.

Select the first point from the good practice checklist above, 'Ensure that the daily routine includes plenty of time for children to play', and evaluate the daily routine in your setting.

◆ *How much time during the day/session do the children have to play?*

◆ *What sort of play are the children involved in?*

◆ *Observe the children at play and compile a list of the skills they are using and developing.*

◆ *Reflecting on your reading of this chapter, what conclusions can you draw from the list you have compiled?*

Adult-initiated play and child-initiated play

There is a vast difference in how the term 'adult-initiated play' is interpreted from setting to setting. Early years practitioners who use it as an opportunity to plan appropriate activities and experiences that build on children's current knowledge are using it as a valuable teaching tool. If adult-initiated play is thoughtfully and sensitively implemented, the opportunities for developing and practising a range of skills is immense. **Moyles** (1999) believed that appropriate adult-initiated play can ensure children learn from where they currently are in their learning and development. However, this can really only be achieved through careful observation of child-initiated play. This would give you a more focused picture of what the child's interests and abilities are.

When children are engaged in adult-led activities they may display a limited example of their skills and abilities. This is because activities that are planned and implemented by the adult often have clear aims and objectives from which children are unable to freely deviate. Therefore they only display the skills required for the activity and not others that may become evident in play initiated by the child.

CASE STUDY:

MOTHER'S DAY DAFFODILS

At Butterfly's Pre-School, small groups of children are busy making Mother's Day cards. The materials have already been prepared for the children by the early years practitioner. Egg boxes have been painted yellow and cut up to represent daffodil trumpets, stalks and leaves have been cut out from green card, and yellow card has been neatly folded in half with 'Happy Mother's Day' written on the inside. One by one the children are shown how to put the pieces together to make a replica of the card made as an example by the practitioner. During the activity, a second practitioner carries out observations of the children at work for their individual records. She notes that most of the children are able to follow instructions given to them but very little else.

1 Why do you think the observing adult was unable to draw more conclusions from their observations of the children during this activity?

2 How could this activity be presented to the children in order to gain a true picture of their skills and abilities?

If you use observations of children engaged in adult-led activities, this may lead to additional activities and experiences being developed that will have less impact on learning.

Findings from observations of children engaged in child-initiated play can be used to inform the planning of relevant activities and experiences that will develop existing skills and encourage emerging skills. Observation has always been a time-consuming undertaking for early years practitioners and one which is vulnerable to losing priority when other pressures and time constraints exist. However, without this vital means of gathering information about children, we are unable to plan play effectively. Sometimes we assume we know children based on what we generally observe. However, specific and focused observations are far more detailed and give a far more accurate picture of the child and their abilities.

CASE STUDY:

PLAYING TOGETHER

Sophie is 4 years 10 months old. She has been attending school for a term and appears to have settled in well. In preparation for parent consultations, the class teacher carries out an observation on each of the children during free-play activities. Through these observations, it becomes clear that Sophie is often on the periphery of play, playing alongside other children rather than with them.

1   Why do you think this has only been noticed through more focused observations?

2   What action do you think the class teacher needs to take?

Observations of children engaged in play enable you to:

◆ ensure safety
◆ identify new patterns and themes of play
◆ be aware of any emerging problems
◆ identify ways to support and extend play
◆ identify opportunities for challenge
◆ get to know each child
◆ make links between theory and practice
◆ demonstrate that we are interested in and value children's play
◆ inform the planning of a suitable and appropriate curriculum
◆ provide evidence of how the children are using the environment and resources.

TRY IT OUT

- *Observe one child for 15 minutes during free play each day for a week.*
  - *Is there a common pattern to what they choose to play with?*
  - *Do they choose to play with the same children?*
  - *What do you think may be the child's current interests?*
- *Use the information gathered from these observations to plan two activities which would enable this child to develop their skills.*
- *How do you use information from observation to inform the planning of appropriate activities for all of the children in your setting?*

The levels and quality of interaction from the adult can have a direct influence on the quality of the play and subsequent learning that takes place. Interactions need to be of a supportive nature, scaffolding learning and taking children onto the next level (Bruner, 1976). **Bruner** also believed that instruction was an important part of the learning process which contrasted greatly with **Piaget**'s theory that identified the role of the adult as a facilitator. **Bruner** argued that the adult should actively intervene to help children construct new knowledge and understanding. Practitioners who sensitively intervene in order to scaffold children's learning raise the quality of play. However you must know when to interact and do so in a meaningful and sensitive way.

Interacting with children at play

Why?	◆ To support children who are having difficulty playing well ◆ To support learning ◆ To extend learning ◆ To provide ideas as a starting point for play
When?	◆ When children request your interaction ◆ When you can see there is a need to interact
How?	◆ In a sensitive and meaningful way ◆ After you have observed which form of interaction is best

CASE STUDY:

THE HEALTH CENTRE

At First Steps Nursery the role-play area is changed every two weeks to allow children to experience a broad range of role-play situations. Currently it is a health centre to link with the settings theme 'The community'. Four children are actively involved in playing in the area. One child is listening to the doll's chest with a stethoscope, another is weighing a number of dolls and recording their weights in a notebook. Two other children are in the 'waiting room' discussing possible diagnoses. Although not all of the children are playing together, they are happily playing alongside each other, using the resources appropriately. Max, the early years practitioner, enters the area and attempts to join in the play by requesting a cup of tea. None of the children acknowledge him and his second request is also ignored. Max takes a seat in the waiting room and fakes illness requesting to see a doctor. Still he is ignored. He remains seated and observes the children at play; however, one by one they leave the area to play elsewhere.

1   Why do you think the children did not interact with Max?

2   How do you think Max could have approached the children differently?

3   Can you think of a situation when you may have interrupted children's play unintentionally?

4   How can we tell when our interaction is not required?

In some early years settings, adult-initiated play is incorrectly interpreted as doing things for children, resulting in activities having little or no value for them. This form of play carries even less value when it takes priority over any other forms of play, minimising quality learning opportunities. The 'conveyer belt' experience of activities is sometimes still evident in some settings where children are called to complete an activity by the adult as they systematically work through a list of children's names. The adult guides the child towards pre-set learning outcomes from which they are encouraged not to deviate. This is most commonly done in order to complete craft activities. The end product of this type of activity is very much the focus rather than the process itself.

CASE STUDY:
CLAY

Once a week, Red class has the opportunity to work with clay as part of their creative activities. The class teacher has planned a programme of activities for the children to do with a teaching assistant working with the clay. The teacher has ensured that her plans have allowed for individual choice and creativity. At the end of the day, the teacher overhears a small group of children discussing the clay lamps made by the class as part of the celebrations for Diwali, which are displayed in the classroom.

'I don't like doing clay' says one of the children. 'I don't like what Mrs Yates makes for me.'

1   Why do you think this child doesn't enjoy working with clay?

2   What is the practitioner doing wrong?

3   Think about how you support children in your setting. Do you do this in a meaningful and sensitive way?

When adults over-support children during creative activities, a sense of ownership is lost and potentially valuable learning experiences diminished. This type of activity has the most learning potential when children freely choose to complete them. When children freely select activities or play experiences, they are more likely to concentrate, develop new and existing skills and see the activity through to a conclusion. **Piaget**'s (1962) theory of cognitive development emphasised the importance of 'active discovery learning' and the child-centred classroom. In practice this means that:

◆ early years practitioners should be learning facilitators, providing children with learning opportunities rather than teaching them

◆ there should be a focus on the process of learning rather than the end product

◆ assessment of children's development is vital so that appropriate activities can be set

◆ activities should be self-motivating for children to engage their interest and further develop skills

◆ activities should be suitably challenging

◆ experiences should be as real as possible (concrete experiences)

◆ practitioners should encourage children to actively interact with each other. In small groups, children can have the opportunity to learn from each other.

The balance between adult-directed play and child-initiated play should be tipped heavily in favour of child-initiated play. The following checklist can help you to assess this balance in your setting.

Structured play

Free-flow play can provide a great deal of fun and learning. However, there is a possibility that some play may become repetitive. By structuring play, you can stimulate, encourage or challenge the child, extending their learning and introducing new skills. Helping children to play requires sensitive and careful interactions on your part.

In structuring play opportunities and activities and by carefully supporting children, play benefits can be retained as more formal learning is introduced. You can model behaviour and ideas in order to enhance learning, for example by demonstrating how something works, acting out a role or making suggestions. You can provide verbal guidance in order to encourage problem-solving.

Spiral play

Bruner's concept of the spiral curriculum, introduced in Chapter 2, page 64, can also be applied to play. Spiral play is the process in which children revisit activities and experiences. It is thought that children's learning is of higher quality when they are able to revisit previous activities, helping to extend their ideas and consolidate understanding. Children have the need to repeat and practise activities in order to consolidate what they have learned. In spiral play, activities are presented in a simplified manner – becoming more complex as children revisit them.

Rich and valuable play opportunities are vital in stimulating and enhancing learning as well as providing you with the opportunity to observe children. Observing children at play enables you to gain an insight into many aspects of their development. The way they interact with each other clearly illustrates levels of social and emotional development. The items they select to play with can give you clues about their current interests and preferences. How children problem-solve during play can give you an insight into their cognitive and intellectual development. These insights are helpful as they not only inform your planning, enabling you to support children's learning, but also validate any assessments made.

GOOD PRACTICE CHECKLIST

Spiral play

Provision exists for children to revisit an experience when:

- opportunities are built into the planning of an activity for children to return to it as they wish
- the same resources and materials are readily available for them to freely select
- time is available for children to freely choose to revisit activities and experiences
- planning takes into account that some children will need to and want to revisit activities more than others
- provision is made for the children to reflect on what they have learnt and how they have learned it
- resources are of a high quality and attractively presented to the children
- practitioners take time to observe the children at play, making any necessary changes to ensure they have the opportunity to revisit activities.

CASE STUDY:

ROSIE'S GARDEN

Rosie is 5 years old and has just started school. She has been totally absorbed in working on a model in the creative area all afternoon. She has used a variety of boxes and materials to create a model of a garden. Unfortunately she is unable to finish the garden before the end of the session. At home time she is given her model to take home. This upsets Rosie as her model is not yet finished and she wanted to work on it again the next day. The early years practitioner explains to her that this would not be possible as they have other activities planned for the next day. Rosie takes her model home but refuses to tell her father about it when he asks.

1   Why would it have been valuable for Rosie to have the opportunity to revisit this activity?

2   Why do you think Rosie did not want to tell her father about her model?

3   How do you accommodate children in your setting who want to complete unfinished work or revisit activities?

Assessing children's learning through play

Wood and Attfield (2005) consider assessment and evaluation as essentially at the heart of teaching and learning. Assessment enables practitioners to:

◆   develop their professional knowledge and understanding of how the children learn

◆   make informed judgements of children's learning and progress

◆   gather information about the effectiveness of the curriculum

◆   reflect critically on the quality of provision

◆   build on and extend children's knowledge, skills and understanding

◆   make links between home, community, pre-school and school

◆   collate information that can be shared with parents and other professionals

◆   evaluate the quality of the play environment.

The play environment

To ensure you provide rich and valuable play opportunities, you need to give careful thought to how equipment is presented and how the environment is organised. The quality of the learning environment is a vital factor in what and how children learn.

Traditionally, settings have organised their space into distinct structured areas, for example the role-play area, small world play, creative area, construction area. The advantage of organising the environment in this way is that it is practical. Resources and materials for each type of play can be presented together. It is also helpful for encouraging children to tidy up after play, as they can easily find where things belong. However, by providing a structured environment play can be restricted and more stereotypical. Children pick up on clues from their environment on how they are expected to behave. A rigid room arrangement with constant reminders from adults not to move resources from one area to another will restrict the flow of children's play.

CASE STUDY:

DON'T MAKE A MESS

Abby is 4 years old and attends Green Park Nursery School five afternoons each week. She is very lively and particularly enjoys physical activities. She has developed some friendships but currently prefers to play alongside others or by herself.

Abby chooses to play with the same ride-on truck every day, using it to move from one area to another, often chatting to herself about what she is doing. For the first time she loads the truck with a handful of small construction toys from each tray in the construction area. She rides the truck over to the imaginative play area and delivers the load at the bakery shop.

'Here's your delivery,' she calls as she tips them out onto the floor in the middle of the shop.

'Thank you. We wanted more things to sell. Our cakes are all gone,' responds another child while carefully sorting the construction toys onto cake trays.

An adult quickly intervenes, calling Abby back to the imaginary play area and asks her to tidy up the mess she has made. She is reminded that toys are not to be moved from one area to another as it makes too much mess and a lot of tidying up.

1   What does Abby's play tell us about her development?

2   What opportunities to extend or develop Abby's learning has the adult missed?

3   How would you have responded to this situation?

You need to view each area as being potentially interactive with each other where possible and permit children to transfer resources from one area to another. This allows for more innovative play. However, safety of the children and the resources will need to be taken into account. Children are very good at using their imaginations and will naturally use one object to represent another if the required item is not available. This is probably most commonly seen with gun play where children will replicate a gun using their fingers or make one out of small construction toys.

CASE STUDY:

BUILDING A BUS

A group of 3 and 4-year-old nursery children are working together to make a bus with the large bricks. When the bus is finished, there is some discussion on what to use for a steering wheel. The bus driver goes in search of a suitable object while the others take their seats on the bus. The driver returns with a large tambourine and sits down at the front of the bus. An adult waves to the children as the bus leaves for the shopping centre.

1 Why do you think these children are confident in using the nursery equipment in this way?

2 How could you encourage this type of play?

3 Which resources do you think are not suitable to transfer from one area to another?

4 How would you make sure the children knew which resources and equipment could be played with in this way?

Rigid and compartmentalised environments send children the message that their play is also expected to be compartmentalised too, restricting their choices and ability to transfer knowledge and understanding from one area of play to another.

THINK ABOUT IT

Drawing on your knowledge, experience and your reading, consider the following questions.

◆ How are play and learning linked?

◆ What conditions are needed to support children's learning through play?

◆ What constraints exist in your setting that prevent you from providing high-quality play provision?

◆ How might these constraints be addressed?

Availability of equipment and resources

Inviting and accessible equipment and resources encourage children to freely self-select what they would like to play with, enabling them to make progress from their own starting point. Pre-selected equipment set out on tables by you prevents children from making choices about what they want to play with. Being able to make choices in play inspires and encourages learning and is a vital component of a quality-learning environment.

CASE STUDY:

UNAPPEALING ACTIVITIES

Jem and Alima run a community playgroup. They carefully plan what the children are going to do each day and set the room up with a range of age-appropriate activities. They routinely select jigsaws and tabletop activities from a small selection and place them on the tables. Recently they have noticed that other areas in the room appear busier than usual and that the children are not choosing to play with the activities set up on the tables.

1 Why do you think the children might not be choosing to play with the table-top toys?

2 What could be the effects on the children's learning?

3 How do you think Jem and Alima should tackle this possible problem?

Toys

As early years workers we recognise the value of what could be described as more traditional toys, such as play dough, building blocks, art materials, small world toys. These types of toys are beneficial for young children in helping them to develop life-long skills, problem-solving and perseverance. Many of the children you work with are exposed to toys that are sold as learning tools. There are numerous toys available now that aim to enhance and fast-track learning. Electronic speaking toys that question children are vulnerable to being used in place of an adult's company. These types of toys can have minimal learning value as children are fed information rather than having the opportunity to explore, discover, experiment and try for themselves. As we have discussed in this chapter, children learn best when they are free to play and explore with the support of adults who are sensitive to the needs of children. It is interesting to note that often you will find the most stimulating toys and resources sold in the least visited aisles of the toy shop.

Play with babies

Babies and very young children explore their environment through their senses. They begin to develop an understanding of how things work or what things can do, making connections with what they already know.

Well planned and organised equipment and resources enable babies and young children to make choices and to revisit previous play experiences. When planning play opportunities, you need to consider how the resources will be made available. Children should be given the opportunity to decide which toy they play with and how they will play with it. It is important that settings think through how to offer activities and experiences to the full age range of children attending the setting. Books need to be presented in baskets or on low shelves, small world toys and figures in low sturdy boxes, simple construction toys easily accessible.

Babies can be given choices by the adult offering two different objects for them to stretch out and grasp, for example a rattle and a soft toy. Treasure baskets (discussed in more detail on page 195) also enable babies to make choices about which object to explore.

For toddlers and pre-school children, settings need to ensure that the range of activities from which the children can choose is interesting and inviting. This will make decision-making a stimulating experience for the children and consequently one they will want to engage in. Occasionally settings store toys out of babies' and young children's reach which prevents them from making choices.

The Birth to Three Matters Framework, discussed in Chapter 1, recognises the benefits of babies having the opportunity to make choices and to learn by doing rather than by being told. The process of making choices and decisions helps babies and young children to develop their self-esteem, which in turn develops their ability to make decisions.

The table below gives examples of age-appropriate games and toys for children under 3 years of age.

Some age-appropriate games and toys for children aged 0–3 years

Age	Example
0–3 months	Wind chimes, mirrors, mobiles, cloth books
3–6 months	Baby gyms, rattles, noisy toys, teethers, feet puppets, board books
6–9 months	Textured books and play mats, soft building blocks, cause and effect toys, balls, board books
9–12 months	Toy telephones, shape sorters, books with flaps, cars, balls, treasure baskets
12–18 months	Simple puzzles, stacking toys, pull along toys, climbing frames and ride on toys, pushchairs and dolls
18–24 months	Musical instruments, tea sets, play house, gardening tools, building blocks, books
24–36 months	Dressing-up clothes, child-sized household equipment, construction toys, puzzles, dolls to undress, books, play dough

Heuristic play

Elinor Goldschmeid's key ideas are based on her concerns with showing how advances in our understanding of child development impact on everyday practice. Her three most important influences on current practice have been:

◆ heuristic play

◆ treasure baskets

◆ the key person system.

The key person system is discussed in Chapter 4, page 134, and Chapter 5, page 148.

Through years of observing young children at play, **Goldschmeid** identified that they have a natural curiosity to investigate. She called this type of play 'heuristic play' which simply means to find out or to discover. She developed activities for 1–3-year-olds based on her findings, providing them with a wide range of non-commercial objects to explore and experiment with. These include:

◆ tins

◆ corks

◆ pebbles

◆ ribbon

◆ buttons

◆ clothes pegs

◆ cardboard tubes.

The role of the adult in heuristic play is to sit nearby and quietly observe. This supports children making their own choices and discoveries. This age group loves to sort, arrange and order objects using their senses to explore and learn. Heuristic play gives young children the opportunity to do this.

Babies also use their senses to explore things and **Goldschmeid** recognised this and came up with the idea of the treasure basket, based on heuristic play. The treasure basket is designed to be used with babies who can sit but are not yet mobile. There are only two rules:

◆ The objects are chosen to appeal to the baby's five senses and must be of natural materials and not plastic.

◆ The adult should sit quietly and not interfere with the baby's play.

The basket itself should only be 4 inches high so that the baby can easily reach into the basket without it tipping over. It ideally should be 12 inches across and filled with plenty of everyday items selected for their varying tactile qualities for babies to explore, scrutinise, mouth and play with at their leisure.

The following table gives examples of the types of resources you could include in a treasure basket.

Contents of a treasure basket

Sense	Example
Touch (texture, weight, shape)	Fir cone, large pebble, shell, large feather, pumice stone, loofah, natural sponge, wooden nail brush, raffia coaster, egg cup, silk scarves, leather purse, velvet
Smell	A lemon, a lime, dried lavender in a cotton bag
Taste	An apple
Sound (ringing, tinkling, scrunching, banging)	Bunch of keys, chains, small metal egg whisk to bang things with, small tins with lids, large dried seed pods, bunch of bells, tissue paper
Sight (colour, form, length, brightness)	Shiny objects as listed above, fabrics with contrasting colours (black and white), patterned silk scarves

You should check the items regularly for safety and cleanliness. The basket should be replenished on a regular basis in order to maintain the baby's interest.

Outdoor play

As an early years practitioner, you should give careful thought and consideration to all aspects of the classroom. Each area should be organised and well resourced. You will work closely with your colleagues and reflect on practice, making any necessary changes. This level of consideration also needs to be consistently applied to the outdoor environment if children are going to regain some of the outdoor experiences they have lost through our changing society.

The outdoor play environment is ideal for providing opportunities for children to:

◆ design, build and construct

◆ take part in vigorous physical activity

◆ experience scientific discovery

◆ develop their language and communication

◆ develop mathematical concepts

◆ use their imaginations.

Most of the pioneers of early education valued the outdoor environment as vital in promoting high-quality learning experiences. Over recent years, the value of the outdoor area has been recognised and much work has been done to improve the outdoor areas of schools and early years settings. However, it is using the outdoor area as a teaching and observing environment that needs to be developed. For outdoor play to be a successful and effective learning area, it has to be organised in a particular way. It should not be viewed merely as an area for children to run around and use up energy in but as a valuable and rich learning opportunity. The indoor environment is well organised so that the whole curriculum is on offer. The same should be applied to the outdoor area, which should be viewed with equal status as the inside environment and should be planned, organised and resourced in the same way.

Bilton identified ten guiding principles for working in the outdoor classroom (see below).

Ten principles for working in the outdoor classroom

◆ Indoors and outdoors needs to be viewed as one combined and integrated environment.

◆ Indoors and outdoors needs to be available to the children simultaneously.

◆ Outdoors is an equal player to indoors and should receive planning, management, evaluation, resourcing, staffing and adult interaction on a par with indoors.

◆ Outdoors is both a teaching and learning environment.

◆ Outdoor design and layouts need careful consideration.

◆ Outdoor play is central to young children's learning, possibly more to some children than others.

◆ The outdoor classroom offers children the opportunity to utilise effective modes of learning – play, movement and sensory experience.

◆ Children need versatile equipment and environments.

◆ Children need to be able to control, change and modify their environment.

◆ Staff need to be supportive towards outdoor play.

Source: Bilton (2002)

The success of the outdoor environment is dependent on the adult's enthusiasm for it. It is the role of the adult to bring the children and both the indoor and outdoor environments together. The quality of this interaction enables the children to function at a higher level (Vygotsky, 1978). Higher levels of functioning are possible when children really have to think through ideas, analyse and work with others to solve problems. As **Bilton** has outlined above, the outdoor area needs as much attention as the indoor environment.

The outside environment enables us to teach children a wide range of skills, including:

◆ handling natural resources correctly

◆ caring for the outside environment.

Summary

It is during play that children show their intelligence, their ability to problem-solve, trying out new ideas. Play enables children to explore the world beyond what they already know, developing their abstract thinking. Play enables children to function at a higher level with sensitive interactions from adults.

The theorists discussed in this chapter all focus on play as a means of learning. They all acknowledge not only children's innate need to engage in play but equally their right to play. They emphasise the importance of learning rather than teaching and recognise that learning should take place through play and not at the expense of play.

There is an overwhelming recognition among early year practitioners that play is more than just recreational or filling time. They recognise the principle that children learn best through play. Play enables children to develop intellectually, emotionally, physically and socially. Well-planned play helps children to develop their social skills by enabling them to:

◆ become more aware of others

◆ become more sensitive towards others

◆ develop an understanding of how other children feel.

As with all areas of practice, it is helpful to be reflective on the play opportunities your setting provides, asking yourself:

◆ What is the quality of the play provision?

◆ How can this be improved?

CHECK YOUR UNDERSTANDING

1   What is play and why do children engage in it?

2   In what way did the pioneers of early years education contribute to the role of play in the education of young children?

3   What are the main differences between the pioneers of early years education outlined in this chapter?

4   Which teaching by the pioneers of early years education does your setting mostly reflect in practice?

References and further reading

Athey, C. (1990) *Extending Thought in Young Children: A parent–teacher partnership*, Paul Chapman Publications

Bilton, H. (2002) *Outdoor Play in the Early Years*, David Fulton

Bruce, T. (1991) *Time to Play in Early Childhood Education*, Hodder & Stoughton

Bruce, T. (2001) *Learning Through Play: Babies, toddlers and the foundation years*, Hodder & Stoughton

Bruce, T. (2004) *Developing Learning in Early Childhood 0–8*, Paul Chapman Publications

Bruner, J. (1976) *Play: Its role in evolution and development*, Penguin

Daly, M., Byers, E. and Taylor, W. (2004) *Early Years Management in Practice*, Heinemann

Drury, R., Miller, L. and Campbell, R. (2000) *Looking at Early Years Education and Care*, David Fulton

Goldschmeid, E. and Jackson, S. (1994) *People Under Three*, Routledge

Isaacs, S. (1933) *Social Development in Young Children*, Routledge & Kegan Paul

Makins, V. (1997) *Not Just a Nursery*, NCB

Maynard, T. and Thomas, N. (2004) *An Introduction to Early Childhood Studies*, Sage Publications

Miller, L. and Devereux, J. (2003) *Supporting Children's Learning in the Early Years*, David Fulton

Mosley, J. (1970) *Quality Circle Time in the Primary Classroom*, LDA

Moyles, J. (1999) *The Excellence of Play*, Open University Press

Piaget, J. (1962) *Play, Dreams and Imagination in Childhood*, Norton

Pugh, G., De'Ath, E. and Smith, C. (1994) *Confident Parents, Confident Children*, NCB

Vygotsky, L. (1978) *The Mind in Society*, Harvard University Press

Wood, E. and Attfield, J. (2005) *Play, Learning and the Early Childhood Curriculum*, 2nd edition, Paul Chapman Publications

Useful websites

For more information on Maria Montessori:

www.montessorieducationuk.org

www.montessori.org.uk

Glossary

Accommodation   Information being processed will not fit the existing schema and the child has to adjust its concepts to accommodate the new information (Piaget)

Adaptation   The process of assimilation and accommodation (Piaget)

Adult-initiated play   Play that is provided for by the adult

Anthroposophy   The study of spiritual science, eurhythmy and nature; a movement based on the ideals of Rudolf Steiner

Areas of learning   Six areas of learning that underpin the Curriculum Guidance for the Foundation Stage

Assimilation   A process whereby the child takes in information and fits it to the existing schema it has in its brain (Piaget)

Atelier   The art studio in the Reggio Emilia approach where the children in a pre-school work with an atelierista

Atelierista   An experienced and qualified artist who is a member of staff in the Reggio Emilia approach

Attachment   Feelings of an emotional closeness between children and principal carers (Bowlby)

Child-initiated play   Play that is initiated by the child that can either be stimulated by the resources present or by their imagination

Connectionists   Researchers who study the co-ordination of the brain

DfES   Department for Education and Skills

Directress   The trained teacher in a Montessori school, so-called as the teacher's role is to direct the child towards learning opportunities rather than teach

Early learning goals   Established expectations for most children to reach by the end of the Foundation Stage

Electra complex   The theory that young girls desire their fathers (Freud)

Emotional intelligence   Awareness of your own and others' emotions and the ability to use feelings to motivate yourself and to develop relationships with others (Goleman)

Empathy Sensitivity to the feelings of other people and the ability to understand their emotions

Episodic memory Exercises and activities to practise recall

Equilibration Being in balance; once a schema has changed and developed, a state of equilibration exists (Piaget)

Eurhythmy Beautiful or harmonious movement

Free-flow play Play in which children are fully engaged and in control of that which provides a network of related processes which include struggle, exploration, manipulation, discovery and practice (Froebel, Bruce)

Ideal self The self-concept that is most desired by an individual (Rogers)

Identification What happens when a child absorbs the beliefs and moral values of the same-sex parent (Freud)

Key worker/key person system Assigning a named practitioner to develop a close relationship with a young child and their parents in the setting, enabling the child to build a strong relationship and to feel secure; the practitioner will be responsible for a small group of children (Goldschmeid)

Language acquisition device (LAD) Human beings are born with an innate ability or pre-disposition to learn language (Chomsky)

Motherese A special and simple language parents use when talking to their young baby; also referred to as parentese (Schaffer)

Naturalistic Observations taking place in a child's natural environment without too much change or artificiality

Non-verbal communication Communicating through physical expression and body language

Oedipus complex The theory that young boys desire their mother sexually, leading to rivalry with their father (Freud)

Ofsted Office for Standards in Education, the inspectorate for education that aims to ensure standardisation of provision

Pedagogista A co-ordinator who acts as a consultant and resource person to several schools and centres in the Reggio Emilia approach

Peer tutoring An older child works with a younger child to help them

Phonology The organisation and pattern of sounds

Piazza The central meeting place found in all Reggio Emilia pre-school settings

Positive self-regard The need to like and respect oneself (Rogers)

Procedural memory Teach by showing and doing, doing something repeatedly in order to remember it

Rhythm A term used in Steiner schools to indicate the flow of activities through the week

Scaffolding Supporting a child to build on things they have already learnt

Schema   A mental structure that enables the child to classify its experiences (Piaget, Bruce)

Self-directed play   Similar to child-initiated play

Self-identity   A person's view of themselves with a possible mix of both negative and positive feelings

Self-concept   An individual's thoughts and feelings about themselves (Rogers)

Self-esteem   Children's evaluation of their own worth including the relationship between what they feel they are and can do, and what they ought to be as a person and be able to do

Semantic memory   Maintain opportunities for discussion about places, facts, events and people.

Semantics   Groups of words and their meanings

Staged theory   Theories that are based on ages and stages as part of development and ability to learn

Stepping stones   Identified stages of progress towards the early learning goals

Syntax   A meaningful combination of words

Transference   Occurs when a person takes the perceptions and expectations of one person and projects them onto another person (Freud)

Unconditional positive regard   To give caring attention without judging or evaluation (Rogers)

Zone of actual development   The stage of development which the child can achieve alone (Vygotsky)

Zone of proximal development   The stage of development the child can achieve with help from an adult or peer (Vygotsky)

Table of researchers, theorists and theoretical perspectives

Please note that this table is not a definitive list and apologies go to any current researchers who have not been included.

Name	Dates (if applicable)	Main area of study	Main features
Lesley Abbot	Current researcher	Early years curriculum, play and Birth to Three Matters Framework	Play promotes learning. Led the team that developed the Birth to Three Matters Framework
Mary Ainsworth	Current researcher	Attachment	Developed the work of Bowlby and separation anxiety
Chris Athey	Current researcher	Cognitive development	Developed and researched the concept of schemas
Albert Bandura	1925-	Social learning	Studied how children learn from role models and how this can influence their learning and behaviours
Alfred Binet	1857-1911	Measurement of intelligence	Developed a series of tasks to measure intelligence in both adults and children
Peter Blos	Current researcher	Development of adolescent identity	Friend of Erikson, adolescence is an important time for reducing the impact of earlier negative events
John Bowlby	1907-1990	Attachment	Looked at the effects of forming strong bonds and attachments, usually with a maternal figure

Name	Dates (if applicable)	Main area of study	Main features
Tina Bruce	Current researcher	Early Years Education and Play	Considers the value of play in early years education, introduced the idea of freeflow play
Jerome Bruner	1915-	Scaffolding	Built on beliefs of Vygotsky but developed the idea that children develop different ways of thinking rather than passing through stages. Considered the role of the adult in helping children learn
Robert Case	Current researcher	Cognitive development	Believes cognitive development is based on information processing theory
Noam Chomsky	1928-	Language development	Introduced the idea of a language acquisition device (LAD) which was instinctive. Can be linked to the nature/nurture debate
A.D.B. & A.M. Clark	Current researchers	Early years experiences	How early experiences can affect but not necessarily determine later development
V Das Gupta	Current researcher	Cognitive and language development	Developing the theories of Piaget and Vygotsky
Margaret Donaldson	1926-	Cognitive development – how children think	Built on the work of Piaget, well-known for her book 'Children's Minds'
Judy Dunn	Current researcher	Language development	Concept of causal talk and the notion of the concept of cause
Erik Erikson	1902-1939	Emotional and personality development	A student of Freud; felt that emotional and social development are linked to cognitive and language development. Personality continues to develop into adulthood. Stages of development are called psychosocial as children explore relationships

Name	Dates (if applicable)	Main area of study	Main features
Jerry Fodor	Current researcher	Cognitive development	Believes that all children are born with identical representational systems that are genetically structured to allow us to make sense of the world
Sigmund Freud	1856-1939	Emotional and personality development	First theorists to consider the unconscious mind and its effect on development. Believed development was stage-like; stages are called psychosexual and are linked to the physical pleasures associated with each stage.
Friedrich Froebel	1782-1852	Early learning through play	Established the first Kindergarten, believed in indoor and outdoor play and placed great value on symbolic behaviour
H Gardener	Current researcher	Multiple intelligences	Worked on genetically determined mental operations
Arnold Gesell	1880-1961	Maturation	Described patterns of development that are genetically programmed
William Glasser	1925-	Needs	Believed in empowering children through non-judgemental recognition leading to a positive feeling of self-worth
Eleanor Goldschmeid	Current researcher	Heuristic play and the role of the key person	Influenced by the views of Piaget, heuristic play stimulates physical and cognitive development. Considered the need for children to have secure relationships with a key person
Florence Goodenough	1886-1959	Drawings as a measure of intelligence	Developed the 'Draw a Man' test with point scoring system
Penny Holland	Current researcher	Physical play, superhero play and war games	Researched the effect of a zero tolerance policy on children's development

Name	Dates (if applicable)	Main area of study	Main features
Michael Howe	Current researcher	Intelligence	Emphasises the role of the environment in changing children's IQ
Susan Isaacs	1885-1948	Value of play and the role of parents	Influenced by Froebel. Believed that play would enable children to have a balanced view of life, and that parents are the main educators of children.
A Karmiloff-Smith	Current researcher	Language development	Proposed that babies are born with a number of domain-specific constraints which help give the child a positive start to life
Lawrence Kohlberg	1927-1987	Moral development and gender identity	Extended and redefined Piaget's views. Suggested that individuals develop moral reasoning in six stages and three levels. Sex roles emerge as stage-like development in cognition
John Locke	1632-1704	Education	Believed that babies are born with everything to learn, 'an empty vessel'
Abraham Maslow	1908-1970	Needs	Developed a hierarchy of needs that follow the life cycle. The hierarchy has five levels and is dynamic, with the dominant need always shifting
Margaret McMillan	1860-1931	First-hand learning, importance of health and social education and free play	Member of the Froebel Society. Believed in training early years workers. Established the first open air nursery
Maria Montessori	1870-1952	Structured play	Believed children have times in their lives when they are more able to learn certain things than at other times
Robert Owen	1771-1858	Early education	Believed that the educational environment was a prime factor in shaping children's learning, social development and behaviour

Name	Dates (if applicable)	Main area of study	Main features
Ivan Pavlov	1849-1980	Classical conditioning	Studied a type of learning where an automatic response such as a reflex is triggered by a new stimulus. Worked primarily with dogs.
Jean Piaget	1896-1980	Cognitive and language development, also play and moral understanding	Introduced the theory of stages or cognitive development, considered how children learn concepts. Also considered stages of play and moral development. Highly influential
Robert Plomin	Current researcher	Genetic influences on development	Recognition of the importance of genetic influences on individual differences between people, adopted children and their families
Carl Rogers	1902-1987	Self-concept development	If the image of ourselves and the image of our ideal self are the same we will develop good self-esteem
H Schaffer	Current researcher	Social development	Social development and aspects of attachment
Selleck	Current researcher	Emotional and social development	The role of the key person and the need to establish secure relationships
Mary Sheridan	Current researcher	Physical development	Established developmental norms through repeated and numerous observations of children
B.F. Skinner	1904-1990	Behaviourist theory	Worked primarily with animals, remembered for the 'Skinner box' and introduced the idea that a behaviour would be repeated if reinforced
Rudolf Steiner	1861-1925	Community education	Believed relationships between children and adults are very important if a child is to develop to their full potential

Name	Dates (if applicable)	Main area of study	Main features
Edward Thorndike	1874-1949	Reinforcement	Followed on from the work of Skinner. Assumed that learning happens due to an association being made between a stimulus and a response and the pleasure/satisfaction that follows
Lev Vygotsky	1896-1934	Social learning	Worked along similar lines to Piaget in that he believed children are active learners, but also upheld that social development is a very important part of cognitive development. Introduced the idea of the zone of proximal development (ZPD)

Index

activities
  appropriate 4, 5, 49, 50
  emotional development 156
  literacy development 95, 96-7, 98
  Montessori schools 175
  reading skills 98, 100
  to support communication 83, 84, 85
  to support schemas 55, 56
adult role 70
  in emotional development 158-9
  good practice checklist 112
  in heuristic play 195
  in outdoor play 197
  in play 180, 183-7
  in social interaction 110-14
adult-initiated play 183-7
Ainsworth, Mary 124-5, 126
analytical phonics 99
anger management 143
attachment 116, 119-27, 137, 159-61
Attfield, J. 190

Bandura, Albert 109
behaviourist approach 176
  language acquisition 74, 75-6, 80
bereavement and grief 150-1, 157
Bilton, H. 197
Birth to Three Matters 11-15, 194
Bloom, Lois 77, 80
Bowlby, John 119-20, 121
Bruce, Tina 52-3, 57, 70, 169
  on communication 85-8
  and language development 90
  on use of symbols 92-3
Bruner, Jerome 62-7, 78, 113-14, 173
  on language development 79, 80
  role of adult 63, 64, 65-6, 70
  scaffolding 63, 65-6, 70, 113-14, 174
  spiral curriculum 64, 67, 70, 188-9

checklists for observation 90, 91
Chelsea Open-Air Nursery School 37
child-initiated play 183-7
Chomsky, Noah 76-7, 80
circle time 170

Clay, M. 95
cognitive development
  activities 44-6
  and language acquisition 78, 80
  Piaget's stages 42-6
cognitive viewpoint on play 180
communicating with children 9, 73-103, 164
concrete operations stage 42, 46
connecting schemas 52, 53, 56
connectionists 87, 103
conservation 42, 45, 46
  test 43, 49
creative play 170
cultural variations 4
  attachment 125
  children's friendships 115-16
curriculum and developmental needs 49, 51
curriculum frameworks 1, 2-15
Curriculum Guidance for Foundation Stage
    1, 2-10
  areas of learning 8-10
  impact on practice 2, 3-8
  outdoor environment 37
  play 179
  principles 2-8
  supporting early language 89

Denham, S. 158
discovery learning 64
Dolya, Galina 60
Donaldson, Margaret 49, 78-9, 80
Dowling, M. 142, 149
Dunn, Judy 115, 131-3
dyslexia 101-2

early years practitioners 67-9
  interacting with young babies 127
  key person approach 134-6
  knowledge and skills 70, 107
  and play 172
  role in emotional development 164
  and transference 136-7, 138
egocentrism 45, 49, 128
Elfer, P. 134-5
Emerson, P.E. 120

emotional coaching 158-9
emotional development 9, 142-64
  acknowledging feelings 149-51, 155
  applying theory to practice 162
  coping with feelings 149, 155-8
  environment for 144, 149
  parenting styles 158-9
  self-esteem 153-4, 157
  self-identity 152-3
  transitions 145-7
emotional intelligence 143-52
emotions and learning 144
empathy, development of 143
English as second language 100-1
enveloping schemas 52, 53, 56
EPPE (Effective Pre-School and Primary
  Education 3-11 Project) 59
equipment
  appropriate 5
  organisation of 7
  play 192-3
Erikson, E. 153
experimental play 170

family variations 114-15
Fawcett, A.J. 102
feelings
  coping with 149, 155-8, 164
  expressing 149-51, 181
Forest Schools 1, 34-8
formal operations stage 42, 46
free-flow play 169, 177-9, 188
Freud, Sigmund 109
  stages of development 161-2
  on transference 136
friendships
  developing 128-34
  identifying 130-1
  and moral understanding 131-2
  observation of 133-4
Froebel, Friedrich 37, 110, 173
  on play 168-72, 180

Gandini, L. 29, 31
Gardner, H. 143
Goldschmeid, E. 127, 134-5, 194-6
Goleman, D. 142, 143, 158-9
Gopnik, A. 87
Gottman, J. 158
Graham, J. 98, 99-100

Halliday, Michael 79, 80, 89
heuristic play 194-6
Higgins, David 60

Hughes, Martin 49

imaginative play 170, 173
impulse control 143
inclusion of children 4, 5
independence, development of 145, 146
individuals, children as 49, 50
interactionist approach to language 79-80, 85
Isaacs, Susan 37, 173-4, 180

Kelly, A. 98, 99-100
key person system 134-6, 148, 160, 194
Key to Learning 60, 61

LAD (language acquisition device) 76, 103
laissez-faire model of learning 110
language development 9, 73, 74
  applying theory to practice 87-8
  behaviourist approach 74, 75-6, 80
  books and stories 93-5, 96
  Bruce's theories 85-6
  by age 83-5
  and cognitive development 78, 80
  contextualisation of 89-90
  and curriculum frameworks 88-9
  functions of language 89-90
  interactionist approach 79-80, 85
  learning grammar 76-7, 82, 84
  nativist approach 76-7, 80
  observation of 90-1, 103
  second language 100-1
  semantic approach 77-9, 80
  supporting 83-5, 103
  and talking to children 95
LASS (language acquisition support
  system) 79, 103
learning
  assessing through play 190
  by doing 49, 51, 194
  environment 7, 45
  frameworks 1-38
  and movement 175
  and play 167, 168-9, 171, 198
  role of practitioner 67-9, 70
  sensitive periods for 175
learning theories 41-70
  Bruner 62-7
  Piaget 42-51
  Rogers 164
  Vygotsky 58-62
listening skills development 143
literacy skills 9
  activities for 95, 96-7, 98
  dyslexia 101-2

supporting children 88-100

McGarrigle, James 49
Macintyre, C. 143
McMillan, Margaret 37, 176-7
Malaguzzi, Loris 26, 28-9
Maslow, Abraham 92
  hierarchy of needs 144
materials
  meeting needs 8
  Montessori schools 16, 17, 18-20
  to support schemas 55, 56
mathematical development 9
Maynard, T. 127
memory skills 87
monitoring progress 8
monotropism 120
Montessori, Maria/approach 1, 15-21, 175-6
  ad play 181
moral development 70, 131-2, 146
motherese 79, 81
movement and learning 175
Moyles, J. 173, 183
music and singing 156, 158

National Curriculum for 5-16 year olds 1
National Literacy Strategy (1998) 97-8
nativist approach to language 76-7, 80
needs 8
Neill, A.S. 110
Nicholson, R.I. 102
non-verbal communication 73
  characteristics of 82
  of infant 118
  in language development 81-8
  methods of 86

observation of children 4, 6
  checklists 90, 91
  friendships 133-4
  language development 90-1
  play 183-5, 188-9
  and responding 49, 50
outdoor environment 34-8
  activities 44
  play opportunities 170, 196-7
  principles for 197
  value for play 169, 173
Owen, P. 152

parent-infant interaction 116-17
  reciprocity 118
  stages of 116-19
  supporting 117-19
  topic sharing 118

parental involvement 5, 149
parentese 79, 81
parenting styles and emotions 158-9
peer tutoring 58, 113
Penn Green Centre 54
Pestalozzi, J.H. 110
phonics 98-100, 103
phonology 81, 82
physical development 10
Piaget, Jean 42-51, 70
  active discovery learning 187
  applying theory to practice 44-6, 49-51
  criticisms of 48-9
  influence on modern practice 49
  on language and thought 78
  on learning 109
  on moral understanding 132
  and play 185
  schemas 45, 47-8, 70
  stages of development 42-6
Pinker, Steven 78
planning activities and Curriculum
  Guidance 3, 4, 5, 6, 7, 8
play 167-98
Pound, L. 143
practical experiences 45, 49, 50
pre-operational stage 42, 45
pre-reading skills 93-4
problem-solving 144
  and play 171-2, 182
psychoanalytical theory and learning 109

quality assurance schemes 8

reading skills 93-4, 97-8
  phonics 98-100
Reedy, David 90, 100, 101
reflective practice 38, 67-9
  and communication 73
  on play opportunities 198
  and transference 137, 138
  using Piaget's theory 49, 51
  using Vygotsky's theory 62
Reggio Emilia approach 1, 26-33
relationships 107-38
  with parents 149
  trusting 147-8
Riddall-Leech, S. 134
Riley, J. 89, 90, 100, 101
Rogers, Carl 162-4
role play 170
  and emotional development 156, 162
romantic thinkers 109, 110
  on play 180

Rosen, Michael 94
rotation schemas 52, 53
Rousseau, Jean-Jacques 109, 110
routines and emotional development 144, 148

scaffolding learning 63, 65-6, 70, 113-14, 174, 185
Schaffer, H.R. 81, 110, 114
    on attachment 119, 120, 121, 123, 125
    pre-reading skills 93-4
    schemas 45, 47-8, 52-7, 70
    activities and materials 55, 56
    adaptation 47
    development of concepts from 57
    providing support for 54-7
security, sense of 148
self-awareness 128-9, 142, 143, 146, 152-3
self-concept 163
self-confidence 160, 182
self-directed play 174
self-esteem 142, 144, 153-4, 157
    and attachment 160
    and play 194
Selleck, D. 134-5
Selman, R. 128-9
semantic approach to language 77-9, 80
semantics 81, 82
sensitive periods for learning 175
sensitivity and attachment 126-7
sensori-motor stage 42, 44
separation anxiety 120, 122, 123, 160-1
Seton, Ernest Thompson 37
settling-in process 160
sharing and turn taking 151, 163
Shining Eyes and Busy Minds 60-1
skilful communicator 13, 14, 88-9
Skinner, B.F. 75-6, 80, 176
    criticisms of 76
    and play 180
small world play 170
Snow, Catherine 79
social behaviour and emotions 142
social development 9
    early interaction 116, 119-27
    friendships 128-34
    theories 109
    transitions 145-7
social interaction
    importance of early 81-8
    learning through 108-14
    role of adult 110-14
    theories of 109
    with young babies 127
social learning theory 109

social referencing 118
social skills and play 177, 198
society, child in 114-15
sociograms 133-4
spiral curriculum 64, 67, 70
    and play 188-9
Steiner, Rudolf 1, 21-6
Steiner Waldorf schools 22-5
stereotypes and use of materials 8
stories and language development 93-5
strange situation experiment 124-5
strong child 13, 14
structured play 188-9
symbols, use of 91-3
syntax 81, 82
synthetic phonics 99

therapeutic viewpoint on play 180
thinking
    activities supporting 46, 49, 50
    and language 174
Thomas, N. 127
tidying up 7, 23, 190
toys 193
    age-appropriate examples 194
trajectory schemas 52, 56, 57
transference 136-7, 138
transporting schemas 52, 53, 56, 57
treasure baskets 44, 83, 194, 195-6
trusting relationships 147-8

unconditional positive regard 162-3

Valentine, M. 28
visual co-orientation 118
Vygotsky, Lev 58-62, 70, 197
    applying theory to practice 59-60
    influence on current practice 62
    on language and thought 78
    on play 173, 180
    role of adult 60, 63, 111-13
    on social interaction 110

Whitehead, Marian 78, 82, 96-7
Whiting, B. and J. 114-15
Wood, E. 190
Woodcraft Folk 37
Woolfson, R. 150
writing skills 96-7
written narrative observation 90

'young writers' strategies' 96-7

zone of proximal development 58, 59, 60, 62, 111, 113, 173